PUTIN's GOLD

DAVID JOSEPH

ALSO BY DAVID JOSEPH

NOVELS

Korea x *2*

Silent Six

NOVELETTES

The Great Hijacking

Putin's Shoot-down!

SHORT WORKS

The Bully and Other Stories

Putin and MH370/MH17

Happy Stories

C-5 On The Ice

Spook 50

Punjabi

Fathers and Sons

Putin's Gold is a work of fiction. Certain incidents described in the book are based on actual recent and historical events, but other than well-known public figures referred by name, all the characters are products of the author's imagination and are not construed as real, and any resemblance to actual persons living or dead is entirely coincidental.

Copyright ©2015 David Joseph

Published by David Joseph Publishing

ISBN-13: 978-1512324419

ISBN-10: 1512324418

Cover design by David Joseph

For Lukas, Clare, and Lance: You will be around
long after I am gone.

For us in Russia communism is a dead dog, while, for many people in the West, it is still a living lion. –Alexander Solzhenitsyn

Author's note

*P*utin's Gold is the third book in the *Korea Trilogy* but more than the last book in a trilogy it is a stand-alone novel. Each book in the trilogy stands alone, although something more can be gained from reading them in order. For example, a chronology of the Kim regime, their personalities, little tidbits, and the like.

Earlier last year—I'm writing this in mid-May 2015—I was writing the second book in the trilogy, *Silent Six*, a novel about rescuing children from Camp 14 in North Korea, when MH370 disappeared. As I researched Camp 14, as well as the Kim regime, I was appalled and outraged by a tragedy that has been around for over fifty-years. Auschwitz existed for five years. Camp 14 is the "Auschwitz" of our generation that we live with and accept. *Silent Six* exposes Camp 14, but many accounts are written about North Korean atrocities and no one notices. When the idea for tying MH370 into my fiction popped into my head, I was reluctant to do it. I was disgusted by the blatant lies of Vladimir Putin in denying Russian troop presence in Ukraine. That is when I realized my obligation to the living outweighs my obligation to the dead, and if I can use current events against evil men, then so be it. I discovered quickly enough that a story tied to mystery was needed more than another thriller novel, and a writer needs one trait above all others—courage. Thus, the signature element of *Putin's Gold* was planted, that is, linking fiction to real world events and real world bad guys.

Prologue

Salvador Allende

December 9, 1994

Vladimir Putin learned the hard way that one must have 100% trust in those close to you. It was his Ukrainian bodyguard that tipped Ukrainian conspirators off. He was very angered, his anger under control from years of experience, but his mind was on fire. *How does 50,000 pounds of gold disappear?* He had not expected trouble on the large gold shipment from Vladivostok. After all, he made previous shipments using his newly formed transport company. The company, he now knew, consisted entirely of Ukrainian nationalists. The gold was somewhere in the Ukraine! The mob and the best ex-KGB men in the Ukraine could not locate his gold. Yet, as he thought about it, he was astonished at the audacity of the crime. What struck him was the sense of constant betrayal from Ukrainians. There was an intense vengeance within Putin that was frightening, but then, he was ex-KGB, trained by the Stasi, and revenge would come in time. The name of the game, as he figured out, was payback. He did not even want to calculate his loss. What stuck in his brain more than the 1994 price of gold, $394 an ounce, was his hatred toward Ukraine. *This is what happens with the changeover from Marxism-Leninism to Crazy-Capitalism. Somehow, someway, Ukraine would pay for his gold. There was no such thing as ex-KGB men.* Putin vowed to himself. Yeltsin knew nothing about the gold train and his dealings with North Korea. Putin's authority and power was broader, more pervasive, because of his new acquired wealth from "supernotes," gold, cigarettes, and guns. The previous gold shipment documentation values were exaggerated; the inflated figures allowed Chul moo, the North Korean Office 39 Director, to wire large sums of laundered (clean) "supernote" money to Swiss banks accounts, thus creating the cover they needed. The exaggeration of documents in a legal business, the buying and selling of gold, permitted an easy laundering operation to move clandestine funds into open-air channels. He profited when Chul Moo profited. He charged Chul Moo 6 percent on money launder, which went back into the purchase of gold, cigarettes, and "supernotes." The Swiss accounts were growing so large Putin diversified into Cayman accounts. The key was having the funds ultimately end up in a bona fide financial Centre. Putin started the process offshore, full success is only achieved when the proceeds are in multiple mainstream reputable locations. This little "gold incident" was merely a bump in the road. There would be more funneling of gargantuan sums of "supernotes" through laundered Swiss accounts, more gold, and drugs, all part of the new Russian criminal syndicate. This was a lesson on Security! One must not forget the past. He was "old school" KGB; his lessons learned about power would provide strength and the ability to consolidate power and enforce will on people in this new system. Truth existed outside people, it was demonstrated in history, individuals must adhere to the state, be crushed by it if necessary. Communism was the vanguard of society, the spear point in the fight for peace. He needed a new transport service and personal security service based on lessons from the past. This time he would handle face-to-face each employee of the new transport and security service, instead of trusting others. He would, as he heard in an American movie, "double-down" on the gold train. In a few years, he would start reaping the benefits of his hard work, his extraordinary profits, and he, alone, would make Russia great again. He called it his Novorossiya Strategy which is bringing the previous Soviet satellite countries back into Russia. With the break-up of the Soviet Union, Russia was now merely a country. His Novorossiya Strategy would restore Russia to empire status. Success measured by barrels of blood, mafia bosses, killing and crippling of generations of saboteurs everywhere; compromised politicians, who bent and subverted laws for the benefit of the state—it was all for a Great Russia.

There had never been a cruise like it. The journey from the Ukraine to Texas was festive. The skipper of the containership was a fervent anti-communist; the thirty member crew composed of Ukrainians belonging to Putin's missing transport company. The talk never stopped, even at night—especially at night.

"We pulled the wool over the Russian's eyes. Our feat must rank as the greatest heist in history!"

"Now the gold is out of Putin's grasp. Only the crew of the *Salvador Allende* know the secret of the missing gold."

Salvador Allende's schedule called for port at Freeport, Texas, the steel and pig iron to be unloaded, the crew given one day to get drunk, find a prostitute, and sleep. The plan was to unload the gold, store it at two storage units in Oklahoma, and sell it five years later over a period of three years. The proceeds used for the new democracy in Ukraine, breaking from the claws of Russian.

John Steinbeck said in *Mice and Men*, "the best laid plans of men go array." The Ukrainian contact for the gold transfer never showed up. The *Salvador Allende* took on a large upload of rice, poured over 50,000 pounds of gold. The load of steel, pig iron, and gold created hairline fractures in two main ship hull beams. The rice upload exceeded the concentrated load limitations by 25 tons and increased the hairline fractures in the main beams. Exceeding max gross capacity, the *Salvador Allende* departed Texas for Helsinki, Finland. In a gale storm and turbulent seas, the rice and gold shifted to the weakest position of the beams, similar to a cargo shift, when not restrained properly, occurring on a large transport aircraft taking off.

The Ukrainians, hung-over from Tequila and a fast fling with "little brown girls" from Mexico, leaned against the railing, watching the lights of Freeport recede in the distance. The men and their secret were heading into darkness and plunged into the darkness of the North Atlantic five days later.

On 10 December 1994, Pararescuemen Master Sergeant Sam Young's tired eyes continually scanned the North Atlantic. Aboard an HH-60 Pave Hawk Helicopter, his crew searched for survivors from the MV *Salvador Allende,* a Ukrainian Semi-containership that relayed distress calls the previous night of taking on water and sinking. After completing four air refuelings with an HC-130, the HH-60 was close to returning to Shearwater Air Base, when Sam spotted a man clinging to a piece of debris, bobbing in the water.

"Tally-Ho! Tally-Ho! Nine o'clock low. Looks like he is alive! I saw him raise his arm," Sam yelled over the intercom. He was tired, but the sight of a survivor gave him renewed energy. Earlier, Sam and his fellow PJ flipped a coin to determine who would go in the water if the need arose. Time was the major consideration that weighed with Sam, he would low-and-slow into the ocean and prepare the survivor for an immediate pick-up. The Pave Hawk attempted descending to ten feet above the sea and slowing to ten knots airspeed for a safe exit for Sam. Wearing a dry-suit and fins, Sam jumped from the helicopter at fifteen knots airspeed and twenty feet above the large swells. The pilot feared dipping the tail rotor into the rolling swells and never reached the optimal ten and ten, ten feet above the swells and ten knots airspeed. The swells were larger than expected.Sam swam to the survivor. "The gold.... all of the gold....we took from Putin is at the.... bottom of the sea," the survivor mumbled to Sam. Sam saw the man was in a state of severe hyperthermia. He continued to mumble as the helicopter hovered overhead, deployed a forest penetrator, and hoisted the two into the HH-60. The PJs administered treatment to the delirious man enroute to Halifax. He faded in and out of consciousness. The sole survivor of the *Salvador Allende* wreck went into cardiac arrest and died as Sam was loading him into the ambulance at Halifax Airport. John Steinbeck was right.

During the 2002 State of the Union address, President George W. Bush declared North Korea part of the "axis of evil." Condoleezza Rice traveled extensively to the region to build support for a tough response by China, Japan, and South Korea. The U.S. plan calculated pressure put on Pyongyang through economic sanctions would force the Kim regime to collapse. North Korea continued conducting nuclear tests, arming to threaten what everyone thought was peace of the world. But, in fact, the arming was meant to keep the country isolated so the Kim regime could maintain "criminal sovereignty" to run its vast billion dollar criminal syndicate. China was reluctant to pressure Pyongyang, fearing a collapse of the government and a mass refugee crises on its border. China enjoyed the status quo of having North Korea as a buffer from the U.S. controlled South Korea. China considered a chaotic North Korea worse than a nuclear North Korea. The bottom line was corrupt Chinese officials were involved in business with the Kim regime. Over $8 billion of counterfeit $100 bills produced by North Korea circulated throughout the world. The quality of the notes coined 'supernotes' exceeded that of the originals. More 'supernotes' circulated in Asia than local currency.

After the September 11, 2001, terrorist attacks, the United States learned resources were available—Mike Perry, TJ Hill, Sam Young, Dave Chen, Missy Yi, and Sumiko Albright, known in a 1984 TOP SECRET memorandum stored in a safe at the White House as the "Silent Six"—that may have prevented the attack. Through information obtained from a wire-tap at a soccer match in London and from the "Kuala Lumpur" summit, the team knew Osama bin Laden's intention of staging a terrorist attack. Going forward, President Obama appointed Mike Perry Director of the Central Intelligence Agency. Powerful men, within the Federal Reserve, decided how to use resources wisely against the growing 'supernote' menace, for stability is the bedrock upon which successful banking rests. September 11 changed the meaning of power—to a degree that allowed nations, in the face of terrorist threats, the ability to apply guerrilla tactics on a global scale. In regards to North Korea, the "gloves came off."

Dave Chen turned his head and looked into Don's strained, bewildered eyes. He could barely see the slits in the Japanese eyes because of the parachute goggles, oxygen mask, and the darkness. Yet Chen knew Don saw him as if it were daylight. Don wore Night-Vision Contact Lenses, a lens that provided thermal vision, a type of night vision for detecting heat signatures. *Times have changed*, he thought, *Don was the new breed high-tech warrior*. But Chen knew enough about men to be able to read the basic types of emotions from body language. He took a step forward and gazed out the right rear door of the KC-10 tanker into the darkness. When the navigator, handpicked specifically for the mission, calculated the exact time and location for exit, he notified the boom operator. After a brief moment, the boom operator nodded thru his oxygen mask covered with a polypropylene ski face-mask and stepped back. From an altitude of 22,000 feet, Chen and the twenty-seven year old Japanese Pararescuemen exited the aircraft. The boom operator closed the door, notified the pilot, and returned to the cockpit. He did not have a clue who the two men were or why they were jumping from a jet onto the Patagonian glacier of Southern Chile. The entire crew signed sworn affidavit's called "purple penny" statements that legally bound them from ever discussing the mission. It was an easy mission to deny because the KC-10 never did airdrop. The exact reason CIA planner TJ Hill picked the KC-10. The aircraft flew on to

Puerto Arenas, where the crew rested overnight. The next day the KC-10 refueled a C-17 that conducted a winter airdrop of supplies to McMurdle Research Station in Antarctica.

At two-thousand feet, the two men pulled the D-ring on their MT-1x parachute and were under canopy by thirteen hundred feet. They landed within ten feet of each other in the trees on a steep slope next to the San Rafael Glacier, part of the Patagonian Ice Cap in Southern Chile. Within minutes, after accomplishing tree descent procedures, they were set-up in position, above an outcropping in the mountain that provided a viewing of the glacier. A small covered gazebo, built by the Chilean Forestry Service, offered a panoramic view of the skyscraper size ice sheets that crashed into the lagoon.

Thirty minutes after sunrise, Seiji Matso, the Secretary General of the Dojin-kai Japanese crime syndicate, walked with a moderate pace, purposeful, to the Gazebo. After sitting down, he removed a thermos of green tea from his backpack. Patagonia was Matso's family destination to escape an assassination. It was the perfect remote location for a man who had powerful enemies. His organization was at war with the Seido-kai and lately powerful underbosses were killed in Japan. The organization even took on the nickname "Dojin Pharmacy." The young businessman had made an extremely lucrative career for himself in the sale of North Korean Blue meth and 'supernotes.' He was an excellent banker and distinguished himself by sophisticated money laundering with some of the world's largest banks. The "clean" money in-turn went into the Japanese real estate and stock market. The two men watching him knew his morning routine exactly. A U.S. spy satellite recorded his daily morning activities for the past two weeks.

From six-hundred yards, Don sighted the laser-guided, semiautomatic rifle with a networked tracking scope that measured distance, humidity, and other ballistic variables. The bullet fired from the rifle was optically guided by the scope. This increased sniper accuracy, making it almost impossible to miss a target. The scope also provided live video uplink to Tsukuba Space Center in Japan. It was a good location for an assassination with a high-powered rifle. The noise from the receding ice resembled thunder—or a gunshot.

Chen watched as Matso was shot in the head. There was no need to run. They skidded down the slope to the lagoon below.

In the lagoon, through another telescopic sight, the Captain of the USS *Seawolf* watched the two figures with interest as they drew near the water's edge. Seconds later, they entered the cold water and breast-stroked around chunks of ice to the middle of the lagoon. The ⅛ inch "chicken-vest" wetsuit worn under the fatigues helped with buoyancy and the cold water. Chen's eyes were caught by what looked like teeth and tusk at the front of the 350-foot attack submarine as it broke the surface twenty-feet from the swimmers. It looked like a black undersea monster, which was exactly what it was. Except it was bigger, faster, quieter, more alert, and more lethal than any other creature in all the seas. Homeport in Bangor, Washington, the *Seawolf* served under the motto "*Beware the Wolf.*"

They ate well on board the submarine. Twenty hours later, the "COB" or Chief of the Boat, the senior enlisted sailor, informed them a helicopter would pick them up in twenty minutes. This they rode to the aircraft carrier, USS *Abraham Lincoln*. An S-3B, Viking, launched from a catapult, flew the assassins to Travis AFB, after drogue refueling with a KC-10 six times over a period of nine hours.

On the next day, Dave Chen was again at work at the Federal Reserve on Market Street in San Francisco. In the post 9/11 world, the Federal Reserve evolved new strategies and a new set of tools for dealing with anyone that threatened U.S. currency. Crossing the International Date Line, the next night Don ate Sushi at the Izuju Restaurant in Kyoto with his mother, Sumiko Albright, the Deputy Director of CIRO (Cabinet Intelligence and Research Office), the Japanese equivalent to the CIA or MI6.

Chapter 1

Kim Jong Un and his Father

November 15, 2000

Kim Jong un, the son of the North Korean Dictator Kim Jong il, stared out the huge window overlooking the Genève Aeroport in Switzerland. He was watching the baggage handlers load bags onto the AN-124, the Russian equivalent to the Boeing 747. His luggage, nine bags consisting of mainly Nike Trainers and NBA memorabilia, arrived by truck from the Liebefeld-Steinholzi English-language International School in Koniz, on the outskirts of Bern.

Suddenly Jong un turned from the widow and spoke in a large voice to Park, his bodyguard. "I want you to learn everything about large passenger planes, particularly the American Boeing planes." A wild look came out of Jong un's eyes, he smiled slightly, and Park recognized the same excitement as when he played one-on-one basketball.

"Yes, Yes!" exclaimed the bodyguard, showing his new gold teeth, his eyes wide, intense, as if given a task of upmost importance from the heavens. A task handed down by Kim Jong un brought tears to Park's eyes, and he vowed to learn everything about Boeing aircraft. Park, who was already looking at aircraft with an enquiring mind, who would have done anything to please him, who asked everyone that played basketball—and everyone who came to his dorm room for chicken and beer—to let Kim Jong un score on the court and praise him for his intelligence.

"The year 2000 I begin studying Physics at the university and will have little time. You can help me. Boeing is the experts, the final authority. Everywhere I travel all one sees is Boeing aircraft. I think the Russians stole their designs." He treated himself to a small block of Swiss cheese from his coat pocket. Jong un's coat had seen better days, but his weight gain from the stay in Switzerland made the coat appear tight and uncomfortable.

"The intelligence and knowledge you possess for a young man of seventeen is phenomenal! The spirit of the 'Great Father' shines more in you each day. Now you will receive a proper education at Kim Il Sung University and on to the Great Father's Military Academy. It is you that will teach me."

"Yes, I know. Sometimes I feel as if he is in touch with me and guides me. Our future—sea and air—awaits us!" Kim Jong un believed he possessed divine powers bestowed on him from his father and grandfather. He was born into the Kim regime and Kim cult. He knew no other role than the direct descendant role. He was told the same thing over and over and played the same role over and over. The role became habitual and spontaneous, and he threw himself into the role of North Korea's savior, hoping to achieve greatness. His faults and guilt would be canceled; sins were excused in a Kim. *Someday the world will see who I am*, seventeen-year old Kim Jong un said to himself in his new man's voice, as he looked at the Antonov An-124. He was enthralled by large planes and ships.

The bodyguard was thrilled by the wisdom Jong un revealed. The hasty departure from Switzerland was good. Outsiders may think the young Kim inferior in his studies, obsessed by basketball, into bondage-themed pornography, or one that escapes from reality by sketching silly pictures. He knew Jong un better than anyone. It was the "sea and air" that obsessed him. I should read *Moby Dick*, he thought, *if the divine one read it twice, I should at least read it.*

In 2008, due to declining health from diabetes, the head of North Korea was grooming his son, Kim Jong un to assume power upon his death. The selection of the youngest son as heir to power was unofficial but his mind was made up. His son was aggressive, a hearty drinker and smoker, and processed the trait of annihilating opponents, an essential skill to ensure the survivability of the Kim Dynasty. Short, with black bouffant style hair, wearing a jumpsuit and giant sunglasses, Kim Jong il authoritatively mentored his son on the guarded secrets of the Kim criminal empire. His eyes were those of a man who appeared a fool, thus he always wore sunglasses. Behind the sunglasses, his eyes revealed suspicion and paranoia. His mistrustful mind worked best in the afternoon, before the effects of cognac took control.

At the Ryongsong Residence in Northern Pyongyang, sitting on the bleachers, after playing basketball, Kim Jong un wanted at this moment to hear nothing else, to think of nothing else, but his father, and the conversation they were about to have; of secrets of the past and advise for the future.

"My strategy of kidnapping foreign citizens falls under Office 35 and the project is called 'Localization.' I started the project in 1972," Kim Jong il said hoarsely at Jong un, and his son turned gratefully in his direction, thinking of a question.

"I thought my grandfather started the project," Jong un inquired.

Kim Jong il only smiles. "No, no, he may receive the credit, but it was my ambition and brainchild," he warned him sharply. "There are three reasons for my 'localization policy.' First, we must have teachers who can train our spies with localized knowledge on their county. Second, it allows identity fraud and permits our spies to gain genuine foreign identities. Third, we can expand our 'seedbearing strategy,' which we are reaping rewards," Jong il said, emerging from a reflection.

"Seedbearing strategy?"

"It is best not to talk too much about this strategy that . . ." he paused, but smiling, clearly pleased. "Yes, an ingenious way to create spies who look foreign, but are born and bred in North Korea. This can be achieved by breeding women abducted. It is also achieved by sending attractive female spies abroad to become pregnant by white men, black, or whatever."

"That will pollute our gene pool. Didn't the Great Father eliminate inferior Koreans in order to keep the genes strong?" *He remembered the Great Father eliminated short Koreans. A sore topic to his father.* Jong un wondered.

Jong il shrugged. He speaks quietly. "That is a good point. Yes, he did. Always remember a problem can always be solved by a bullet. In the case of the offspring, Office 35 ensures they spend their entire lives in strict apartheid." Jong il lit a new cigarette with the end of his last one. "I was going to hold off telling you...but I think it best that you know as much as I know about my most secret project." His voice sounded weak, hardly his own voice, as Kim Jong il was paranoid discussing the topics with his son.

Kim Jong un felt his blood temperature drop a few degrees. "I serve you father" was the automatic reply. His face revealed nothing of his feelings.

For a moment nothing happened, and then Kim Jong il threw the cigarette on the floor. He sat where he was for the moment, panting and looking around the gym, before whispering. "This must not be talked about to no one other than your uncle, Chul moo, the Director of Office 39 and Minister of State Security," Jong il observed in a quiet voice. "If information leaks it will mean failure, perhaps war. For that reason, I do not concern myself with details. Without the details, I can honestly deny the operation."

"Why Chul moo?"

"Chul moo is an operational genius. He masterminded our success with the 'supernotes,' forcing the Americans to change their currency. He is the mind behind Office 39. He is a Kim and the only man you can trust. I repeat, he is the only man you can trust. Is that understood? He is permitted his own large secret police unit to protect Office 39 and the Kim Family."

"Yes, father."

"It is an aspiration of mine to pull off the perfect Hijacking of a passenger jet. The Great Hijacking!" I task Chul moo with this job eight years ago. He has a plan in place."

"Why?"

"Many reasons," he began, "all good reasons as long as it is the perfect hijacking. The reasons will benefit yourself more than me."

"I fail to understand father. But of course I believe you."

"The Americans have built a fence around us. The U.S. State Department has labeled us a terrorist state. We are not linked to, or known to have sponsored, any international terrorist attacks since 1987. After the Trade Center Bombings, Bush labeled us part of the' axis of evil.' The Americans box us in a corner and muzzle us.

This weakens us as a power. We must show the Americans and the world we can climb over the fence whenever we please."

"Muzzle us?'

"A muzzle means you can't bite. We are getting off track somewhat. As I said earlier, the perfect hijacking will benefit you more than me."

Jong un was seized with doubt. "How?"

Jong il noticed his son's confusion and knew he needed to directly get to the point. His voice was benevolent. "When I am dead you will fill my place. You are young. Your enemies will try and assassinate you. The enemies are within North Korea. You will need to execute hundreds around you. At the same time you must pull off a spectacular international event. This will raise respect and fear in your enemies. That is why the hijacking must be a close guarded secret."

"The world will condemn the hijacking and further isolate us."

"You are right. Your head will be on the chopping block if this operation is not done right, but if the hijacking is flawless and perfect, in time, the Americans, Russians and Chinese will know what happens when you are muzzled—you bite! The code name is *IO* and only Chul moo and a few agents are aware of the operation. *IO* means Indian Ocean. The world will think the aircraft sank to the bottom of the sea in the Indian Ocean. The plane will land at Pyongyang. The details concerning the aircraft will remain a mystery. It will be like that hijacking mystery in the United States that everyone says, 'what ever happened to DB Cooper?' To this day the DB Cooper incident remains a mystery."

"How will the incident raise respect and fear if no one knows?"

"There is no perfect crime or perfect anything for that matter. As the years go by, someone will defect or some little evidence or rumor will surface implicating us. The CIA will secretly pinpoint or suspect we are involved. It will only be speculation and suspicion. This will raise your leverage and standing in negotiations, and the like, on matters like nuclear weapons," Kim Jong il told his son, "Anyways, you can always deny the allegations. We deny allegations all the time with border excursions, midget submarine operations, and various other incidents meant as provocations with the South."

"I am beginning to understand. You have my curiosity."

"For the most part, allegations against us deal with incidents isolated to the peninsula. As a new, young leader you will need an incident of a global scale to raise your status and prestige with the powerful nations. But the incident must be perfectly executed! For now, I will give only limited information you need to know. Operation *IO* is a very sophisticated and well-planned mission. It may take years waiting for, as Chul-moo says, 'the stars to align.' As a world leader, it is best not to know intricate details. Chul moo is the best and he is your only ally. That is enough information for today," sighed the father, rolling his dark eyes heavenwards. Just as he was getting ready to stand he suddenly muttered, "Oh, there is one little point about this mission that I find remarkable!"

There was dead silence as the two stared at each other. Jong un broke the silence. "What! Tell me father."

"Three of the agents involved in the recruitment and handling of the pilot who will one day fly an airliner to Pyongyang are all products of my 'localization' and 'seedbearing' projects!"

A gleam came into Jong un's eye. *Because of the work of my father and grandfather, I have a head start on becoming a Great Leader!*

Chapter 2

Spy School

With the turn of the century, the year 2000, Kim Jong il tasked the Office 39 Director, Chul moo Kim, with the additional duty of running Office 35. He did this for one reason only and that was for Chul moo to plan, organize, and execute the perfect hijacking. "I want you to do for Office 35 what you have done for Office 39!" Kim Jong il told his adopted brother, Chul moo. The world contained a small number of sick souls of whom Chul moo happened to be one. His new job, on his simple view, was to create the ultimate spies to conduct the perfect hijacking. The master of the 'supernote' regarded his added duty of taking over Office 35, as a new form of idealism. As the years went by, he embarked, with fascination, on the challenge of turning North Koreans into Americans. What started as a job of creating a few Malaysian and Singapore spies, turned instead into overhauling the entire Spy School. The North Korean (DPRK) Spy School, a place where men and women (often boys and girls) disappear without a trace and all evidence of their ever having existed disappear with them. Chul moo's dangerous energy, diverted into a sinister game of engineering humans.

The Koreans, along with the Japanese, are one of the most homogeneous races on the earth. Therein lies the problem for the North Korean spy—ethnicity. Kim Jong il addressed the spy ethnicity problem by the abduction of foreigners from other countries. Starting in 1972, he kidnapped citizens from various countries around the world and brought them to North Korea. He called it his 'localization' policy. A special compound, surrounded by barbed wire, housed the kidnapped foreigners who became instructors, teaching localized knowledge of their homeland. In addition to instructors, the foreigners assisted Kim Il sung with his new policy called 'seedbearing.' This policy was the breeding of instructors to produce off-spring to be raised from birth to become a spy. In 1994, Chul moo, while involved in acquiring new technology for his 'supernote' operation in Silicon Valley, came across information called In vitro fertilization. In vitro or IVF, from the Latin meaning in glass, is used because early biological experiments involving cultivation of tissues in glass containers. IVF sparked a new interest for Chul moo, who envisioned within twenty years of having a "test-tube spy" for every major nation—anywhere where a Caucasian can pass for a native—he would have North Koreans burrowing into the fabric of these nations. Using 'supernotes' and help from the KGB, Chul moo recruited a lab technician from a leading fertility clinic in Walnut Creek, California. Through the lab technician, he acquired eggs preserved by oocyte cryopreservation, along with sperm from various different races. A new compound, within Camp 14, surrounded by barbed wire, staffed with technicians in lab coats and clad in elasticized hospital slippers, shuffled on the linoleum. The man that created the 'supernote' was engulfed in a mad experiment to create the 'super spy.' In addition, Chul moo decided to upgrade the training and standards at the Spy School.

Jasmine and Lily, two Malaysian women abducted from a small coastal village in Malaysian by North Korean agents when they were six years-old, just completed the third day of their final exam for Spy School. For the past three years, the two attended a grueling program at Keumsung Military College. Even the three years with the People's Army was nothing compared to the three years of rigorous training at Keumsung required for all North Korean Intelligence agents. Thousands of people trained at the college, but the Intelligence agents were trained in a secret valley apart from the main campus. Intelligence was a nice way of saying government sponsored murder and mayhem. The two took tests the entire day covering philosophy and the history of Kim Il sung. It was not as strenuous as the ten mile run through an obstacle course that they ran on the first day. Upon completion of the ten mile run, the recruits were tested on martial arts. Every student, at a minimum, obtained the rank of First-degree Black Belt in a combination of Hapkido and Tae Kwan Do. The final test was full-contact defending yourself against three attackers. On the second day, the weapons and driving skills test was administered, all part of the physical portion of the exam. The weapons test included sniper rifles, pistols, archery, knife throwing, and explosives. Their driving skills were tested with a Mercedes at high speeds through an obstacle course of poles, sheets of ice, and hairpin turns.

The last part of the final exam was a field test, which simulated an actual mission an agent may encounter. Jasmine and Lily were paired up on a scenario to infiltrate an embassy, memorize documents written in English from a safe, and return—without being detected—within a four hour window. The scenario included a mansion surrounded by a walled compound patrolled by guards and dogs. For the test they were given a paintball rifle, two pistols, two knives, a rope with a grappling hook, a stethoscope, glass cutters, a floor plan of the mansion, and lock picks.

After completing the testing, it was determined that Jasmine and Lily both passed with high scores. The two would never forget the words told to them after receiving their test scores: "Tomorrow you will meet Director Chul moo Kim. Good luck."

In January 2010, Jasmine and Lily was visited by Chul moo, who arrived early in the morning in his black Mercedes stretch. Chul moo was escorted into the library by the school commandant, and the two were so startled by his sudden appearance that they almost fell from their chairs while standing up.

"Comrades," said the commandant, "this is the Director. He wishes to speak to you."

They both bowed low at the waist. Chul moo exchanged a few words with the commandant, whom he seemed to know well, and then the commandant departed, leaving the three alone.

"Comrade Jasmine, Comrade Lily," Chul moo greeted them sternly, offering his hand. "It's good to see you. I understand you both graduated at the top of your class."

"Thank you, sir," they both replied, accepting his hand shake.

"Sit down," he said. Chul moo removed a Browning Hi-Power 9mm handgun with a thirteen-round clip from his jacket and a knife. He set both items on the table before the two agents. "Your target is two books on my command." He moved around the library slowly and deliberately, withdrawing two books from the shelf. He spun around, holding a book in each hand, off his left and right side. "Fire!"

Simultaneously, within a second apart, one book received the pointed knife while the other book received a bullet, both in the center of the book. "Very good," Chul moo said, walking over and sitting down at the table with the women. "Comrades, I will start with the end in mind. Your mission is to assure a Malaysian Airlines Boeing 777 is hijacked and flown to the fatherland." He paused, while watching the two.

Jasmine and Lily both were nervous and did not know what to say.

"This mission, for your ears only, was conceived by Our Dear Leader, Kim Jong il. He assigned the mission of executing the perfect hijacking to myself. I personally planned the intricate mission details. The most crucial detail of all will fall to you two. You will recruit a senior pilot, that we have identified for his vulnerabilities, to fly the aircraft to Pyongyang. Again he paused to emphasize the gravity of their task.

That Kim Jong il initiated the mission himself indicated the importance of their orders. Jasmine took a deep breath and looked at Chul moo, who was watching her in turn. "Mr. Director, I will not fail."

"Nor I," Lily said firmly.

"This mission is the most important undertaking intelligence has ever attempted. The survivability of the entire nation may depend on it. I estimate that it may take three to five years before mission execution. After the mission is completed you both will be national heroes."

On hearing his words, the two new agents grew more and more excited. Finally, after years of training, they were going into the field on a high-profile mission!

"Jasmine, you will be set up with a travel agency in Kuala Lumpur. Lily will go to a travel agency in Singapore. From this time forward you will deny knowing each other. Yet your mission intertwines. Experienced agents will meet you at your destinations, set you up, and brief you more specifically. There is no need to go into details at the moment. You both will be given five thousand American dollars for expenses." He paused and looked into four eyes. "What do you have to say?"

They both held his gaze then popped out of their chairs and spoke the same words, "I serve the Dear Leader. I will not fail."

"I want you ready to depart with me to the airport in twenty minutes," he continued. "Just a small bag is all you will need. I will be waiting in my car."

Chapter 3

Operation *PG*

April 10, 2011

The photographs taken by the USS *Jimmy Carter* brought ecstatic response in Washington from Perry, the new Director of the CIA, appointed by President Obama; Rear Admiral J.D. (John David) Harris, the head of naval intelligence and a veteran submariner; and Captain Pat Williams, the assistant for undersea warfare in the Office of Naval Intelligence in the Pentagon. There were some 5,000 usable *Jimmy Carter* photos showing the sunken *Salvador Allende* cargo ship. What the *Jimmy Carter* photos showed was two pieces of the wreckage of the *Salvador Allende* lying on its starboard side in 14,000 feet of water in the North Atlantic. The ship had snapped in the middle, due to zone-load limitations exceeded by excessive weight—50,000lbs. of gold—and fell to the ocean floor. Significantly more important than the wreckage photos was the photos of the gold bars hidden in the mud on the sea bottom. The gold bars poured out of the ship when the *Salvador Allende* snapped in-half.

"Gentlemen, as you know," said the CIA Director, his eyes on the forty-six inch screen, "I am an Army man. Can you explain the details, in layman's terms, concerning this operation?"

"I'm sorry about you being an army man," laughed Admiral Harris, almost coughing. "The USS *Jimmy Carter*, a *Seawolf*-class submarine, is modified for special missions of a classified nature. The modification includes a large area I like to call the 'garage'. The garage can be used for various missions. In this case, it was used to launch and recover an *Avin*, a DSV or deep submergence vehicle. The *Avin* took the photos and found the gold through a sophisticated sonar device. The same way, let us say, used to find a 'black-box,' from an aircraft."

"How long has this technology been out there? The ability to recover items from extreme depths," Mike Perry inquired, as he studied the materials sent over from the Office of Naval Intelligence. He had only had a brief time to review the information, looking for relevant data, due to other matters concerning the hunt for bin Laden and drone strikes in Yemen.

"Do you mind Admiral?" Captain Williams asked soothingly.

"Please, Captain, by all means, you are the best qualified man in the navy to fill the Director in on 'our little world' under the sea," said Admiral Harris. "As the CIA Director, you will have numerous operations of the highest level ongoing with us submarine boys. The CIA and submarines are like circles within circles. We certainly need to develope trust with one another—which can start now."

Captain Williams turned to Director Perry. "I think 1965 was a key year. The chief scientist and head of the Deep Submergence Systems Project (DSSP) began a highly classified or 'black' Air Force-Navy program to identify and recover objects from the ocean floor. The objects were often Soviet satellite packages, weapons, as well as similar dropped objects by the United States. Why of course the goal was to recover the item before it sank to the sea floor. The navy along with the Air Force Aerospace Rescue and Recovery Service did an outstanding job during the cold war years. The DSSP constructed two deep-submergence search/recovery vehicles that could operate to depths of 20,000 feet to locate and recover small objects." As Captain Williams looked at Director Perry he realized the man did not have the time for details concerning the history of deep-sea recovery. He continued. "To make a long story short, this work expanded to the Defense Intelligence Agency (DIA) and the scientific advisory board and together we improved and refined our deep-submergence vehicles. We have come a long ways from the CIA Project *Azorian*, the salvage of the Soviet ballistic missile submarine K-129 from the North Pacific," concluded Williams, using the name of a relatively well-known joint CIA/Navy recovery operation.

Perry did not have time to intellectualize any longer, to analyze further. "I want you gentlemen to head a project to recover the gold from the sea floor. The operation will be masked as a civilian commercial oil and mineral exploration. The project will have absolutely nothing to do with the *Salvador Allende*. Can you do it?"

"How much gold are we talking about?" Admiral Harris asked.

"50,000 pounds," said Perry calmly. "And of course the operation holds the highest security classification."

"What is the name of the operation, Director?" Williams asked.

Perry smiled. "Hell, that's easy. Operation *PG*!" The excitement in Perry's voice was obvious.

"Whose gold is it? Harris asked. "And what do we do with it?" *Director Perry might be the Director of the Central Intelligence Agency,* thought Harris, *but he was taking something from somebody and he needed to know who. He ran some math in his head and estimated the gold worth well over seventy billion dollars!*

"The gold will go to the Federal Reserve Bank vault in New York."

"*PG*? Parental Guidance? How the hell did you come up with the name *PG*?" Harris asked the Director, thinking he could zero in on the name to acquire gold ownership.

"*PG*, a highly classified name and project. *PG* stands for Putin's Gold....Admiral, you never answered my question. Can you do it?" The Director asked, his voice firm.

"Hell, that's easy, piece-of-cake, Director!" Williams whispered so loudly it could have been a roar. "From now on, I want you to call me JD."

Alone in his office, the memory of having the 9/11 hijackers in his grasp at the "2000 Kuala Lumpur" summit haunted Mike Perry. He closed his eyes and remembered the day in Kuala Lumpur when he walked away from his team, he liked to call them his team, and returned to Washington. TJ wanted to kill the "would be" hijackers there and then. The agency made an agreement with the Malaysian Special Branch Intelligence unit to only acquire and share the intelligence gathered. *If only he would have given his "blessing" before walking away, September 11th would not have happened. The wars in Iraq and Afghanistan might not have happened.* His reading glasses rested on the desk. Tonight he looked every one of his sixty years. Since accepting the appointment of heading the CIA, he had aged.

Two files lay open on his desk: one, a file on the firm location of bin Laden and assassination scenarios and two, details surrounding the criminal empire of North Korea. But he did not look at the files. Instead, he sipped Scotch, neat, in a glass, and thought of his team's ages. TJ is sixty-nine, maybe seventy, still going strong. Missy, the Deputy Director of the Korean CIA is fifty-four. Sumiko, the Deputy Director of CIRO, is around the same age. Both women held in the Deputy Director roles because of Asian attitudes concerning a woman leading an intelligence agency. Sam Young, the head of the Country Analysis Division with the Federal Reserve and a Pararescuemen in the New York National Guard, was fifty-two. His sidekick and brother-in law, Dave Chen, ran the Counterfeit Division of the Federal Reserve out of San Francisco. The two knew that Mike played a key role helping them gain employment with the Federal Reserve. What they did not know was that it was Director Casey, the 1984 CIA Director that secured their role within the Federal Reserve. Contrary to what most people thought, the Federal Reserve was a private institution and not part of the government. The Federal Reserve welded immense power with little or no restrictions. Sam and Dave both were veterans of the recent wars in Iraq and Afghanistan. They kept abreast of new technology involving special operations. Mike Perry's arch nemesis, Chul moo Kim, Sam Young's identical twin brother, was now a diplomat involved in nuclear weapons negotiations. Mike believed he actually was the de facto ruler of North Korea. Kim Jong il was sick the majority of the time and defaulted all decisions to Chul moo. The "million dollar question" was who would succeed Kim Jong il upon his death. His analysts predicted Chul moo as the successor; however, Sam predicted the young son Kim Jong un. Mike put his money on Sam's prediction. At last, a door to his right, next to his encased Special Forces green beret, opened, and a man with a Glock 22, stepped into the office.

Seconds later, TJ Hill entered. He sat in a leather couch across the desk from Mike.

"Thanks, Chris," he told his body guard. "Why don't you go grab a bite to eat in the cafeteria? I'll text you when I'm ready."

As the door closed, Mike poured TJ a shot of Scotch on the rocks. "Good to see you, TJ." He looked at TJ. "Christ, we're getting old."

Mike's first encounter with TJ Hill was during the "Tree Cutting Incident" in 1976. TJ was one of the PJs on the HH-3, Jolly Green, helicopter that responded to airlift the wounded and dead from Panmunjom to Camp Yongsan. Mike met TJ a few days after the incident at Osan Air Base. Mike was on loan to the 314th Air Division Intelligence Branch to assist with fallout and repercussions from the ax murders. TJ was in and out of the Intel shop and everyone knew him well. TJ's knowledge and insight of the Korean peninsula impressed Mike. TJ spoke fluent Korean, his wife was Korean, and he had been at Osan since 1968. Mike and TJ formed a tacit alliance working on the same goal—the destruction of the North Korean regime. Mike learned through the ranking Air Force Intelligence Officer that TJ received three decorations from South Korea for heroism. These awards dated back to 1968, and it was rumored TJ helped track down North Korean infiltrators involved in the "Blue House Raid." Over the years, their relationship would grow. *TJ is the most amazing and unusual man he had ever met in the military—he was a one-man war,* Mike thought.

"The older the buck, the harder the horn," TJ said while smiling like a mischievous little boy.

"Yeah," Mike agreed uneasily. "TJ, do you remember the gold Sam told us about in Kuala Lumpur?"

"Sure, the *Salvador Allende.* I remember. Why?"

"Well, we are going to go get the gold. But that is just a side note. We are also going to get bin Laden. That is why I wanted to see you. I've reviewed the different scenarios on the operation. I trust your opinion and input. After all, you pretty much built the Special Operations Command single-handed. I want you to go down to MacDill and look over the op. You have their respect and they are expecting you."

"How good is the information this time, Mike? One hundred percent? Ninety?"

"TJ, I want you to go to MacDill. What is going on with North Korea? Talk to me," Mike said evenly, sipping the Scotch and ignoring TJ's question.

"Do you remember 'Red Robin,' the flamboyant All-Star basketball player?"

"Yea, he played for the Chicago Bulls in the mid-nineties. I enjoyed that time in the NBA. It seemed like you had real ball players then. Players that loved the game. Why?"

"He is going to Pyongyang to play in an exhibition game. It appears the young Kim, Jong un has a fascination with the NBA. It was apparent when he went to school in Switzerland. I would not be surprised if the two met in Europe at an exhibition game or something. You know, when the kid went to school. Seems Red Robin will play for the young Kim every year. He has an exhibition itinerary scheduled out for the next few years. Trivia." TJ thought for a moment. "Red Robin started a small company producing whiskey. Anyways, what is on your radar?"

Mike finished the Scotch and turned to the task at hand. Mike pushed the two files aside, rubbed his eyes, and picked up a Sony remote control. A picture of Kim Jong un was produced on the forty-six inch screen. Suddenly, a thought, an ingenious plot came into his head. Like a computer that could multi-task, Mike continued his conversation with TJ while plotting another mission.

"I believe this is the next leader of North Korea. I want you to learn everything about him. On your hard drive is a file of everything we know about him. Most of the information provided by Missy with the KCIA. He has three main weaknesses: women, alcohol, and food. Missy actually believes he has an eating disorder, that is, he binges himself on Swiss cheese, fried chicken, and beer. If that is true we can plan something around this vulnerability. We expect a period of turmoil and uncertainty when he secedes his father," Mike added grimly.

"Kim Jong un may be a long shot."

The DCIA said, "Maybe, but he is the horse we are betting on. I want you to come up with a covert assassination plan—a two to three year plan. It will be executed within the first few years of his assuming power. A time when many around him wish him dead."

The DCIA and TJ studied the picture on the screen, Mike's eyes staring at something only he could see. Mike stopped and stared at TJ. "Can you do it?"

"All right," TJ said cautiously. He sipped his Scotch. But TJ could only shake his head, unsure what to say. The DCIA nodded, as if TJ had agreed completely, and then he began to speak again.

"As to what is on my radar, Putin and Chul moo have a close relationship that is kept 'under the table' very well. It scares me," the DCIA said.

"It should scare you. Chul moo is a 'Pit Bull' on a leash. You know that better than anyone. Remember the 'man with no eyes' that Chul moo killed in Toronto?"

"How could I forget? His name was Bodinko."

"He was Putin's right-hand man that helped Chul moo set up the 'supernote' operation, which is the root of most of the no-good throughout the world. 'The man with no eyes' set up the overseas accounts linked to Putin," TJ stated.

"The Canadians deciphered the Bodinko journal and you will not believe the details." He looks at TJ's head, that final dead glare, then looks away, mouth twitching. "It is fucking unreal!"

"We talked about the journal in Kuala Lumpur. The information was encoded by Hockey games or something." TJ senses new information regarding the journal. "Talk to me boss," he said.

"Funny you mention Bodinko, TJ. Anyways, the Russians and North Koreans have built an absolutely huge criminal empire. Both are huge networks that are growing larger, and I think a threat to the free world," Mike said. "In Russia, through Putin's leadership, a Krysha exists. A Krysha is an umbrella of protection that includes the government, military, police, customs, and border guards. The FBI has identified a clear relationship between Russian organized crime groups and the Sicilian Mafia, the Chinese Triad, and the Yakuza, to name a few. North Korea is a small criminal-syndicalist state, but what we are seeing in Russia is a huge, full-blown criminal-syndicalist state."

"The Canadians must be holding back all the contents in the Bodinko Journal."

"The Japanese are on top of North Korea, more so than us. We have looked into this more after 9/11. Money laundering is investigated deeper now. The criminal enterprises in Russia exist side by side—and often overlaps—legitimate Russian business. The Krysha includes connections to large banks, deep penetration into local and national government, and into the armed forces," Mike said. "Our prediction is the longer Putin stays in power, the more his criminal state will grow. Eventually, he will have no choice but to regain lost soviet territory. As these countries become democratic, they realize the truth, and want to crush the organized crime. Ukraine will be the first territory Putin will pull back into Russia."

"I can envision the scenario of Putin taking out the Kim regime to cover his ass over 'supernotes,' gold, weapons, drugs, and whatever other no-good they are involved in together. I cannot see Kim Jong un, as a leader, lasting over five years. Putin is extremely dangerous. If you want the nitty-gritty on North Korea you need to talk with Sam Young over at the Fed. Sam has been busy while you have been climbing the ladder."

"Oh, I have talked with Sam and Dave Chen. Are you aware the North Koreans are anticipating a 'supernote' of the new hundred dollar bill?"

"No, I thought the new bill with all the embedded security was impossible to counterfeit. The bill is not even out yet. When is it due to be released?" TJ asked.

"Well, they have their sights on the new note. I am not sure when the release is. Sometime in 2013, I believe," Mike says. Sweat runs into one of his eyes, stinging, and he wipes it away like a tear.

"Okay, well it is a damned dangerous world with the two of them in bed together. Dangerous for the young Kim should he inherit a relationship with Putin that is bound to go sour. The Kim regime is a House of Cards, and I know what you are thinking . . . ."

"That we don't need to kill this guy because someone else is going to get him. Actually, the chances are someone within Korea will knock him off." TJ said, looking down at the Scotch in his glass. "You got that right. All Putin has to do is snap his finger and you have a hijacking, bomb on an airliner, or whatever. Putin will use Kim as his 'Pit Bull' more before he 'bites the dust.' That is the real danger with North Korea, not the nuclear weapons. The North Korean nuclear weapons is a smokescreen for the Kim regime criminal syndicate."

At last, the Director sighed. TJ was not telling him anything he did not already know. He would have a talk with Sam before he briefed the President on the new bedfellows. "All right, I want you in MacDill. Get back with me."

They exchanged a look across the years.

The DCIA sighed and rubbed his eyes again.

"And when you finish at MacDill I want you to take a fishing trip."

TJ stood and left the office.

Alone again, Mike leaned back in his chair, contemplating what TJ said. *'Red Robin' was new information. So was hijacking and bomb on an airliner. TJ must have something "up his sleeve." He must know or suspect something. A 'special operator' like TJ does not have casual conversation with the Director of the CIA, even though they have known each other since the 1976 "Tree Cutting Incident" in Panmunjom. Hell that was thirty-five years ago. I'm getting old.*

Chapter 4

RED ROBIN

June 22, 2012

The eight time NBA rebound champion had never had a business opportunity to match the potential of this new one. With malice, he contemplated what his old Chicago Bulls teammates would think . . . unending jealousy, wealth beyond their imagination . . . a guaranteed future in the lucrative beverage market, regrets for not partnering with him. The retired NBA All-Star player hoped to use his previous notoriety and name recognition to market whiskey called "Red Robin."

During his ten years playing professional basketball, Billy Becker was the most flamboyant, outspoken, and outlandish player ever in the NBA. Tall and physically impressive, he made the NBA Defensive player of the year three years in a row. With his red hair, freckles, and pale Caucasian features, Billy distinguished himself from other NBA players. The fans called him "Red Robin" and he liked the name. Along with the name, the body piercings, and the constant clash with opponents and officials, Billy became a sport celebrity or novelty with the public and media. He was the only redneck in the NBA. He took great pride in that fact, since the NBA was seventy-eight percent black. Ironically, Billy only dated black women. He still drove a custom-built, four-wheel drive, ruby red, luxury Ford pick-up truck with a 3 x 5 foot rebel flag flying from the pick-up bed. It was his third red truck since leaving the NBA. After three failed marriages, a short career in the WWF (world wrestling federation), and numerous failed business ventures, Billy felt optimistic about his new distillery in Little Rock, Arkansas. The Japanese were interested in "Red Robin" whiskey, along with maybe the North Koreans. The new leader of North Korea, Kim Jong un, whom he met at an exhibition game in Europe, invited him to play at an exhibition game in Pyongyang, and he intended to talk business with the young leader. Billy had been out of the limelight for years and enjoyed the renewed media attention his controversial visit gathered, as if his presence in North Korea were a delicate matter with potential international diplomatic complications. Billy's cell phone made the noise of a basket swishing through a hoop, his text message said, "Mr. Becker arriving in ten minutes." It was a message from his new Chinese investor.

A narrow alley ran between the rear of Red Robin Distillery and the Little Rock Mortuary opposite the distillery. One end of the alley opened onto California Street, some hundred feet from the distillery door. On the door was the Red Robin logo, an image of Billy Becker holding a basketball. Noticing several lighted basement windows, Dave Chen, head of the Federal Reserve Counterfeit Division, knocked on the door. He couldn't help thinking about Alfred E. Neuman, the fictitious mascot and cover boy of Mad magazine while waiting for a reply. The peephole flap swung back.

"Zhang Wei, Macau Investments," Chen said, and stepped back from the door.

Billy studied him for what seemed an inordinately long time. Then he said, "All right," and unlocked the door, and removed a 2 x 4 from across the door. The door opened wide. Billy looked his visitor over, said, "Come in," and stepped back a step. Chen entered the distillery, and Billy locked the door, putting the 2 x 4 back across the door into the brackets.

"Is there a lot of crime around here?" Chen asked.

"No, no, I just like to be safe," Billy lied.

He accompanied Chen to his office next to a wire caged storage area. The office was filled with the overpowering aroma of whiskey.

Billy looked exactly like the Red Robin logo. He sat behind his desk. He was wearing white sweatpants, a muscle shirt, and untied basketball shoes. His red hair uncombed, his eyes were crinkled in a smile, and his teeth were very white. He looked humorous and drunk, a man without a worry in the world.

Chen didn't comment on the fact that Billy was mildly drunk. He looked at him and said, "Mr. Becker, let me begin by saying that we like your business model and specialty brand whiskey."

"Thank you."

He continued, "After thinking about your business, and after consulting with my partners in the investment group, we have decided to provide 'seed' money for your business."

But Billy did not respond. In fact, Billy had screwed up in business dealings so many times, and knowing he was slightly drunk, he was saying as little as possible.

Chen sweetened the conversation by saying, "This will be 'seed' money in the tune of $25,000." He set a brief case on the desk and opened it up, exposing the neatly wrapped $100 bills.

Billy said nothing for a few seconds, then pointed out, "Zing, I will not let you down. You chinks always deal in cash?"

"That is Zhang, not Zing," Chen corrected him. "No, normally we do not deal in cash. It is because of your unofficial visit scheduled to North Korea. You see the State Department does not approve your visit or allow business dealings with North Korea. We do not agree. That is the reason for the cash."

"Screw them clowns! Kim Jong is a close friend of mine. I like him. I can do what I please."

"We agree 100% with you and applaud your initiative and bravery. Through businessmen like you, new markets open up. We have our sights on the Chinese market," Chen replied.

"The Chinese market?"

"Yes, the Chinese market. The investment group is impressed with your contact with the new leader of North Korea, Kim Jong un. Our research indicates that if you can crack into the elite communist structure, then the wealthy elites will follow."

"What do you mean?"

"Billy, there can be a role for you in this visit. The role of diplomacy and opening markets. You see, every time you visit you give "Red Robin" as a gift. The elites in North Korea are tied into the elites in China. Within three to five years Red Robin' whiskey will be everywhere in China."

"Wow! I never thought my little business could grow into a huge company."

"Well, the most probable scenario is the big boys will buy you out."

He speculated that for a moment, then said, "I am willing to work in whatever way I can with your group. Money talks and bullshit walks. There has been too much bullshit in my life. I will let your money talk. Agreed?"

Chen reached across the desk and shook his huge hand. "Agreed." Chen reminded him, "This business, unlike all our other businesses, is Top Secret and on a need-to-know basis between my group and you." He further reminded him, "You will not discuss, disclose, or divulge anything that pertains to our 'under the table' dealings with your company. And of course, there will be 'seed' money coming your way so long as you keep playing ball and spreading goodwill with Kim Jong un."

"Got it. This opening of markets may be my role, my purpose." Billy reached into a desk drawer and removed a bottle of Red Robin. He poured themselves a little whiskey, to celebrate appropriately, and to wish Macau Investments a long relationship. Or at least long enough for him to become a millionaire.

Chapter 5

Zane

October 9, 2013

By nine o'clock on an autumn weeknight, Hangar Nine, a small bar close to Changi Airport, was beginning to get crowded. The streetlamps turned on accentuated the cleanliness of the Singapore sidewalks. Malaysian Airline Captain Zane Bahmad, still dressed in his airline uniform, imagined a group of flight attendants joining him for a drink. Flying in the cockpit jumpseat, he just arrived on a short flight from Kuala Lumpur. He was in Singapore for three days instructing Singapore Airline pilots in a Flight Simulator on emergency flight procedures for the Boeing 777 aircraft. He "moonlighted" four to six days a month with Singapore Airlines as an instructor in the flight simulator. His company approved the work and it actually improved relations between the two carriers. Moreover, the arrangement established himself as one of the leading triple seven pilots in the world. In reality, he needed the extra money the sim job provided. Captain Bahmad, Zane as he liked to go by, was financially overextended and deep in debt. He understood clearly the reasons for his financial woes. A wife with an extravagant taste and penchant for credit cards, his own habit of acquiring girlfriends in major cities, and his love for alcohol and gambling. He liked to say it was "wine, women, and song" and flying that he lived for. Zane loved flying so much that he never considered himself having a real job. At age twelve, he started as a line boy at a small Kuala Lumpur airport servicing planes. This started him in flying lessons and by age sixteen he acquired his private pilot's license. Before joining Malaysian Airlines, he flew wherever and whenever he could. From fish spotting to traffic reporting, to aircraft delivery, flying is flying. For Zane, the beauty of flying is you never stop learning. He learned something new every time he flew.

But there was no flight attendants advancing for a romantic chance meeting with him. He did drink, however, and he had been drinking steadily at Cloud Nine since six that evening. Zane was nursing his gin and tonic when he noticed the attractive woman at a side table at the other end of the patio bar. She was alone. On her face was an expression to which Zane had become exquisitely attuned. She did not like being alone in a bar and tried not to show it.

Zane paused for a moment, feeling the familiar male-drive of lust . . . though every time he gave in to desire, the feeling grew more intense the next time. The first time he gave in to infidelity he hadn't slept for three days. He always thought about the small Thai flight attendant who called herself Mai, kept wondering how she was doing after all the years. The second time had been easier . . . and the third time more easier . . . and by the fourth time he fell asleep like a baby reliving his encounters and looking forward to the next one.

Zane pulled his credit card from his "hand made in Japan" wallet and motioned for the cocktail waitress. He had one of the exclusive airline Captain's club card that Singapore Airlines provided for expenses incurred during travel. That card was worth its weight in gold, because a bill never arrived at his home address, provided it was used only during his stay in Singapore.

After the waitress took a drink order from the woman, who was looking toward him in surprise. Yes, Zane thought, she was alone all right, maybe twenty-six to twenty-eight—just very alone. Through the streetlamp glare thrown over the patio the woman looked gorgeous, not just gorgeous but physically in-shape. Zane recognized that look when he saw it, because he'd seen the same look in women of different nationalities all over the world over the last twenty years or more.

When Zane moved across the patio, he lowered his chin slightly, and then lowered his eyes, and the most profoundly sincere smile spread over his face.

Lily looked at Zane and gestured toward a vacant chair, and a conversation began, led by Zane himself, followed by the DPRK intelligence agent, with a Pakistani busboy cleaning tables.

"You are Malaysian, yes," Zane asked in Bahasa Malaysia, the standardized form of the Malay language. He sat down in the chair.

"Yes, I grew up in Malacca. And you?" She replied in Malaysian English. Throughout Malaysia, English served as the medium instruction language for math and sciences in all public schools. Lily also spoke Mandarin in addition to Korean.

"Kuala Lumpur. What brings you to Singapore?"

Lily smiled. "My husband owns a travel agency. I work out of the agency. It is boring. You are a pilot!" Lily's eyes opened wide. "That's impressive."

"I enjoy it."

"Why did you become a pilot?"

"Well, as a kid I started out working at a little airport and one thing led to another. And here I am flying for the big boys."

Lily thought back to how she was groomed for the intelligence corps. She too started young and one thing seemed to lead to another.

The two talked through dinner and then shared one ice cream sundae. The check arrived and Zane paid it with his club card, leaving a generous tip.

"How about you joining me for a drink at my hotel?" Zane asked, but his heart was pounding very hard and fast. Part of it was the "thrill of the hunt," as he called it, part of it was fear of the uncertainty he saw in Lily's eyes, most of it was power.

"Sure, if you promise to keep a secret." The seductiveness came out in her eyes.

"All right," was all he said, "I promise."

Chapter 6
Vladivostok

January 10, 2014

The meeting between Putin and Chul moo happened in Vladivostok, and the location resulted from geography. Good location for the Office 39 Director because it was close to North Korea and his travel did not attract attention. Over the years, the location became their regular meeting place. Putin enjoyed traveling across the expanse of Russia, often he would unexpectedly just stop at a small airfield in Siberia to show his presence. Siberia was the "Wild, Wild, West" of Russia and a great place for filming him swimming in a cold river or riding a horse. The Vladivostok trips became similar in nature, that is, he was greeted by two attractive local women offering him the "Bread and Salt Ceremony." Afterwards, he would visit the naval port, home of the Pacific Fleet and intelligence hub for the Far East. He used this trip to congratulate the navy on *Joint Sea 2013,* the largest Pacific joint maritime exercise ever conducted. The exercise was conducted with the Chinese Navy and received close scrutiny by the Japanese and Americans. The trips reminded Putin that Russia was a grand empire that stretched across the globe. His meetings with Chul moo were always at night at his favorite seafood restaurant overlooking the Golden Horn Bay, or what he called Peter the Great Gulf. *I should start renaming and redrawing the map, particularly on the periphery of Russia. I'll start on that after the Olympics next month,* he thought.

Tonight was a special meeting between the two because each had important information to share. From under eyes that seemed to never blink, he studied Chul moo sitting a few feet from him at the small table. When Putin smiled, the eyes did not. After the meal, with formalities over, the conversation began.

"How is the new leader Kim Jong un doing?" Putin asked.

"It has been over two years since the death of Kim Jong il and he is close to securing his power base. Together we have purged the government of traitors and spies. There is one final task we are close to executing and that is why I wanted to meet you. Out of courtesy, I want to inform you of an operation I planned." Chul moo watched Putin's face.

This got Putin's attention and curiosity. This was the man that executed the 1983 Burma Bombing and got away with it, the man that assassinated the Director of the Korean CIA and got away with it, and the mastermind behind the "supernote." Putin showed no reaction. No reaction at all. As if he still waited for Chul moo to speak. Then he blinked. "I'm listening."

"We are going to pull off what I have coined 'the Great Hijacking.' We have a Boeing 777 pilot with a major carrier out of Kuala Lumpur that will fly the jet to Pyongyang. I've worked every detail into the op to fool the world into thinking the plane is flown into the Indian Ocean by a rogue pilot!"

"Putin inhaled deeply and gave Chul moo a small smile. "I believe you. Why? What is your motive?"

"It began as a vision of Kim Jong il's. He wanted to accomplish the hijacking for two reasons: one, for survivability of the Kim regime and two, to gain leverage and respect from the Americans. As his health deteriorated, he task me with the job of planning a perfect hijacking. He already determined the young Jong un as his successor. Jong il knew the challenges the young leader would face, or I should say threats from within the country. In order to secure a power base, Jong un would have to purge the party of undesirable elements and execute a grand international event." Chul moo looked across from where he sat at the table as he picked up his beer. He immediately saw the concern on Putin's face. "What is it, Vladimir?"

"Chul moo, I hate to arrive at a conclusion without knowing operational details. But an international hijacking would isolate and turn the world against Kim Jong un." Putin thought rapidly. *He needed details. How can this incident play into my hand?*

"The one criteria that Kim Jong il insisted on before his death and the same detail Kim Jong un insist on is the operation must be a perfect hijacking. I have worked every detail from the black box, the satellite tracking, the ground radar, to the actual disposition of the aircraft and passengers. Eventually, the Americans may recover an exact reverse engineered black box from the Indian Ocean." Chul moo stopped and stared at Putin.

"You have a triple-seven black box? Pilot? You have a rogue pilot willing to hijack the jet?" Putin moved in his chair and rubbed his small chin.

"I have a team of two female operatives that have been groomed since they were small girls for this mission. In the airline world, there are always pilots that are financially and psychologically challenged. Through data bases and good agents, we selected, let me say, a vulnerable pilot. The 'honey trap' is set, and, Vladimir, if you saw my agents you would understand how helpless a psychologically impaired man will fall,"

Chul moo said, marveling at the ingenious plot.

"Amazing! The black box?" Putin asked, smiling at him brightly, indicating he was interested.

"Office 39 produced ten black boxes. And the Chinese gave me the access codes and instructions allowing our hackers to penetrate key western defense systems tied to satellites, particularly the tracking of aircraft and missile launchings."

As Putin considered the possibilities, he raised his gaze, remembering his information for Chul Moo, and looked out at the lights across the ice-locked bay. It was a breathtaking view in the summer, no matter how many times he had seen it. There were the huge ships of the Pacific Fleet and the commercial cargo ships. Then came the piers, docked ships, and waterfront buildings.

"There is no perfect crime. Eventually someone will find out, which brings me to what I wanted to tell you. Do you..."

Chul moo cut him off in mid-sentence. "Exactly! That is where the leverage I mentioned earlier comes in. The Americans may suspect but will never be able to prove it. They will understand that we can bite! In fact, they will think twice when sitting down at negotiations with us."

From the dim shadows, Putin studied his longtime friend. "Do you remember the gold I lost in 1994? The gold I bought from you?"

"Yes, your newly formed transport company took possession of the gold for delivery. I remember."

Jokingly Putin replied, "Well, I found the gold. As it turned out, the gold was put on a Ukrainian ship. The ship sank in the Atlantic," Putin said, the humor already gone. "Do you know about the Soviet *K-129* submarine?" he suddenly asked.

"No," Chul moo replied. He was very surprised: this, gold, was a completely unexpected development.

"The technology and lessons learned in 1974 from raising the *K-129* from the bottom of the North Pacific paved the way for the recovery of my gold."

"The Americans got your gold?" The Korean's voice crackled faintly.

"Over two years ago. We placed a bug in a key CIA office. It was not easy to place and as it turned out not easy to recover. The gold is in the Federal Reserve vault in New York. At today's gold price that is around One Billion, 40 million dollars." Putin stared at his dinner companion. "Chul Moo, at the Sochi Olympics, I am going to ask for one billion dollars back from the Americans. I decided if I do not get the money I will teach the Americans a lesson—one it will never forget. I think you can help me."

"You know you can count on me," the Office 39 Director replied. "I have another piece of information I wanted to tell you in person. I think this information will help you hit the Americans back for taking our gold."

"What is it?"

"I have, or should say Office 39, produced what I call the 'PBF,' the perfect Ben Franklin!"

Putin raised his beer mug. "A toast! Just like in Berlin where we met and started our joint printing operation!" Again he held up the mug and with much excitement the two clinked glass together. "I want you to relay word to Kim Jong un that I would be honored if he consider a joint business, Russian/Korean, venture in Gold mining. Mining technology has advanced tremendously and together we can tap into your gold reserve. We can finalize the agreement in Moscow in the future. I am just 'sowing the seed' right now. And my good friend, I may need your 'honey trap' team in Europe. If you don't mind."

"Europe? I can add a German operative to the operation. A German girl that was born and raised in Korea. She knows the team, they went to school together, and together will made and unbeatable team."

"Chul moo, you are an intelligence genius!"

"Brost! Like Berlin, when we were young!" Chul moo's words, though spoken with excitement, had the effect of the Vladivostok cold wind.

Chapter 7
Lily & Jasmin

February 2, 2014

Some savage instinct now took hold of Zane, a root fear he could not define. In his life, he had been exposed to dangers like engine fires, smoke in the cockpit, or a landing gear that failed to deploy. Yet Zane considered his current situation as "extreme stress." The stress never stopped because it dwelled in his mind constantly. Whenever he thought of his wife and marriage he missed Lily, who was back in Singapore. Zane was angry at himself for giving in to his newest lust—Jasmin. He regretted laying eyes on her, let alone sleeping with her. He was offended that she could sit before him, beautiful and alive and self-obsessed, while demanding information about the Boeing 777-200 for the Chinese government.

Zane stared at Jazmin, but Jasmin was peering into Zane's mind. "Did I mention I have a sex video of myself, the 'third-party,' and you. Remember the little ménage a trois right here in your own city . . . well," Jasmin said, "I think you better provide the Dash-1 on the 777-200. It would be the first step in putting an end to this whole ordeal."

He would not look at Jasmin, who was staring at him; Zane slid a 2GB flash drive across the table to Jasmine.

"I think we both know how much you enjoyed the threesome, Zane," Jasmine said, "Here is something for your efforts, and I think it will relieve your stress." She extended a brown manila envelope before Zane.

Zane looked into the envelope filled with bundles of $100 dollar bills. *Oh, my god*, he thought, *there must be thousands. The Dash 1 isn't even classified. They could have probably downloaded it from the internet.*

"There is $25,000 there. There is more where that came from if you are willing to take on a part-time job—for a start. My government is interested in various flight simulations run on a computer, an in-home flight simulator—that's all I'm saying—if that's an attractive prospect." Jasmin looked at Zane; they stared at each other.

"Right," Zane finally said.

"Of course, there are 'fringe' benefits that come with the deal. No cameras!" Jasmin said heartily—but Zane looked away from her, as he chose to look away from the likelihood of that. "If you change your mind," Jasmin said, standing up, "You know how to find me." She left the café, and Zane with the money—too quickly for Zane to come to grips with his emotional lows and highs.

Jasmine provided the money for the state-of-the-art computer system with software for the Boeing 777 use in the flight stimulator. Through his connections with the aviation community, Zane purchased the items. It was the combination of flying, money, and sex that produced a new, weird hybrid personality in Zane. His pilot skills, along with his reputation among the airlines, were every bit as well-honed as any other time in his career. Then Lily showed up unexpectedly in Kuala Lumpur from Singapore and the denigration of Zane, the pilot, the family man began.

Jasmine noticed Zane with Lily at a café. Zane could see she was surprised. He saw the terrified look from her—that son-of-a-bitch, as if she were saying, "well, after everything I've done for you." Zane made it appear as if he did not know Jasmine.

"I think that woman knows you," Lily told Zane after she left. She watched her storm across the street.

He laughed. "Crazy bitch! I think she is a flight attendant that wanted to date me years ago," he said. Zane was chilled sitting in the café. He had a momentary vision, terrible and clear, of coming home and his wife confronting him over his current affairs; the airlines wanting to fire him over the "sex videos."

As crazy as it was he met Jasmine and her friend at a hotel that night. In the blackness of the hotel room, Zane experienced three orgasms. The thermostat kept the room cool constantly, but soon the three were sweating. Their bodies glistened—even seemed to glow—in the moonlight. The bed gave off heat. Their bodies slid. Zane said he never experienced such erotica. Then Jasmine and her transgender friend began dressing. He watched the two of them; they were not smiling.

"Is something wrong?" Zane asked.

"I'm done with you. I'm going to China," Jasmine said, and gave Zane a note when she kissed him on the cheek. The man beside her smiled.

"It was fun. Thanks for the ride. My twin brother would have been proud of me," the transgender from Thailand smiled at Zane. The two left the room.

The man reminded him of a Thai Flight Attendant, a translator with Malaysian Airlines, and Zane remembered the note. As a plane took-off from Kuala Lumpur Airport, Zane read it: *your wife has the video. My government told me to give it to her.*

Zane's wife was a private woman in the midst of menopause, and when she saw him enter the house she screamed. He tried to comfort her by saying, "It's all right, it's all right," as he attempted to hold her. She cuddled in the corner of the living room, wondering who the man she married was. She began to see through him.

"What were you going to do if I had not found out?" She asked him. "You would still be doing your 'deeds,' when would it have ended?"

Throughout the week they talked and it was decided that Zane would move out of the house within the month. They would file for a divorce. He could no longer see anything clearly. Even while flying he could not concentrate. Yet to other airline employees, he thought and acted clearly. He had no vision and began drinking excessively.

Zane moved into a small apartment with Lily, who decided to leave her husband to spend her life with Zane. The only item he removed, besides a few clothes, from his home was one computer with the flight simulator software. He left another computer and flight simulator, the one with his island landings, in hope that his son may take up flying. Somehow he believed his wife would get over it and want him back, despite that every time she saw him she laid crying and told him that she could never forgive him. It was over and as the feelings sunk in Zane began to think of ways to kill himself. The shock of his wife struggling financially bore into him like a wound. The only reason he did not commit suicide was he knew life insurance would not cover death from suicide.

Lily tried to comfort him, but he just sulked in his misery. The whole time he was with Lily, he was borderline suicidal. And one evening when he came into the apartment, Lily introduced him to a man, a North Korean that presented a hijacking plan to Zane. As he explained the justification for his government's actions Zane was not even listening. What he saw beyond the man's hand gestures and speech was an honorable way for his wife to receive his retirement, insurance, and a life for himself in a small mountain villa with Lily, who was two months pregnant.

"A dream come true!" Lily called it. She looked at Zane with big round eyes.

Zane spoke for both of them when he said: "Just tell us what to do, sir—we'll do it."

"Okay," the older Korean man said. "We have some flight preparation and training you can do on your home computer. Nothing you can't handle." He took a deep breath and began explaining what they were.

Chapter 8

Sochi

February 14, 2014

On February 14, 2014, while Vladimir Putin drank red wine in the courtyard at the USA House, the U.S. Olympic Committee Headquarters, at Sochi, TJ met with his Russian counterpart, within eye distance of Putin and his twelve-man security detail.

"Thank you for coming on such short notice, TJ. TJ is that correct? Is that the name you go by?" The ex-KGB colonel asked. He looked like an everyday grandfather, not a career KGB counterespionage spook.

"TJ is fine. I bet you are a colonel," TJ answered, looking around as nonchalantly as he could.

"Impressive TJ! I do happen to be a retired colonel. I am now merely an advisor, like you. I am very much like you, an old buck. What is the saying, 'the older the buck the harder the horn?' Does that sound familiar?"

"Once a KGB Colonel always a KGB Colonel," TJ said. *They bugged Mike's office*, TJ thought with surprise. *The gold! That is where the conversation is going.* TJ saw a man not far away in sweatpants, wearing the Russian Olympic uniform, holding a duffel bag with see-through mesh at the end of the bag. His name was Victor Slepynin and Victor Slepynin was FSB (Federal Security Service of the Russian Federation). "It is Okay Colonel, we are filming and bugging this meeting too."

"TJ, I do not know what you are talking about." He held an envelope out for TJ. "TJ, here are open-ended tickets for any event you want to see. Good seats. I hope you stay and enjoy your visit. Maybe it will come down to us and the Americans for the gold in Hockey. That is really what everyone would like to see. What do you think, TJ, about the gold?" Genuine interest in the man's eyes, but not smiling.

"I am sorry. I don't take gifts from adversaries. Colonel get to the point. What do you want?"

"Adversaries? Why we knew about your bin Laden hunt. Down to every detail. We never leaked the information. Now is that an adversary? Look at President Putin 'breaking bread and drinking wine.' TJ you are still in the cold-war. Times have changed."

"Times have not changed. The bear is out of hibernation, and the bear is hungry!"

The chit-chat stopped when the colonel pulled a cigarette pack from his pocket. He fished a note out of the cigarette pack and looked around. . . .

"Putin wants the gold back. Here is the contact to a Swiss Bank. He is very generous in that he only wants an even one billion dollars. Why you can keep millions yourself for the recovery, expenses, or to line your own pockets." He handed the note to TJ.

TJ inspected the note. "A very generous offer." He scribbled a few words on the note. "Give this back to Putin."

The colonel read the words TJ wrote: *Finders keepers, Losers weepers*! "Is this the position of your government?"

"Yes."

"This is going to get interesting. We may take the leash off our Pit Bull. It would be a pity if events spiral out of control—like an airliner disappearing. You will bear the responsibility," the colonel said, rather pointedly.

TJ's face changed. "Good day, Colonel, I hope the hockey does get to us for the gold. It will be a 1980 repeat." TJ made his way past Putin and the security detail. Putin turned his head to TJ. Their eyes met. While looking into Putin's eyes, TJ had but one thought—*KGB*.

TJ entered the Olympic Park and sat down, and immediately became lost in his thoughts. *Dictators that answered to no one ran most of the world. The bear is back.*

Chapter 9
Zane's Last Flight

March 9, 2014

*O*n 9 March 2014, a triple-seven (Boeing 777-200) passenger jet, carrying 239 passengers, took off from Kuala Lumpur International Airport at exactly 0050 hours. The Boeing triple-seven aircraft was piloted by Captain Zane Bahmad, a 53 year-old veteran examiner pilot with over 18,000 hours flying time. His First Officer was a 27 year-old junior co-pilot that simply went by the name Abe, whose boyish good looks conceal a razor sharp mind. Zane was pleased to have a competent sharp co-pilot in the right seat, particularly since the last few days his own behavior and judgment was unusually odd. Abe processed the expertise to operate the Boeing 777 on his own. He could not remember ever being so careless—and so nervous—at the beginning of a flight. Zane had a good reason to be nervous because he planned to commit two crimes— murder and hijacking. The thought of that—murder and hijacking, replaced by the green glow of the cockpit lights—made him shiver.

"Passing ten," Abe said, meaning passing 10,000 feet altitude.

Zane nodded to Abe and reached up to turn the "Fasten Seatbelt" illumination light off. "Good job, Abe. Your pre-flight and engine start checklist was flawless."

"Thank you sir. I wish I tagged along with you in the avionics deck when you did your walk-around. I am not very familiar down there. Hey, thanks for letting me do the take-off," Abe said. "Are you okay? You don't look good."

"Nothing that a little oxygen wouldn't cure. When we get up to level-off and clean up our checklist I'll suck on a little O2. Thank you for asking. Let me jump back and grab my reading glasses from my jacket pocket." Talking made Zane nervous. Zane disconnected from his seat belt and went to the back of the cockpit to get his glasses. The cockpit was dark with the exception of the glow from the instrument lighting on the dashboard.

"Do you want me to flip the light on?" Abe asked. Abe knew some pilots maintained strict light control to aid with night vision.

"No, no, I want to keep my night vision," he answered as he dropped his glasses. While picking up his glasses, Zane pulled the circuit breaker on the ACARS system. He maneuvered over the center console back to his seat.

From engine start, Zane listened to all the radios, UHF, VHF, and HF. Normally, the pilot had one frequency turned up, the radio he was using at the time, while other frequencies were turned off or down low. Listening to all the radios made for a frenzy of communication in his left earpiece. On climb-out after take-off from Kuala Lumpur, Zane heard the call, thought faint and mixed with a loud squeal, "*370* disregard, repeat, *370* disregard." Zane immediately pushed the stopwatch function on his Breitling watch. This was the code word from the North Korean agent in Singapore that two U.S. Air Force KC-10 tankers, call signs *Orca 01* and *Orca 02*, and eight F-16s were airborne from Singapore en route to Misawa Air Base in Japan. *Timing was critical*, Zane thought, *I must kill the co-pilot, disarm the aircraft communications, speed up while descending, and join the radar pattern of the Tankers refueling the fighters.* He was a mission focused professional, instinct and training took over, forcing out any doubts. This was a man that constantly developed and refined triple-seven flying procedures. He had run the rendezvous mission profile many times in his simulator.

"Oh, we have an ACARS malfunction," Abe noted, as he looked at the small yellow illuminated light on the overhead warning panel. He pulled his checklist out and began looking through the pages.

"It is a circuit breaker. We will run the checklist on level-off. This tail has the reoccurring problem passing 30 all the time."

"*MH370*, maintain 350," Malaysia ATC said over the radio.

"*MH370*, copy, 350," Abe replied. He looked over and saw Zane nonchalantly putting on his oxygen mask. This slight distraction delayed Abe from immediately answering ATC. Then he saw Zane reach down and turn off both transponders with a flick of the wrist. Abe was dumbfounded by these actions and about to say something when ATC called again.

"*MH370*, please contact Ho Chi Minh City 120.9, good night."

Zane reached for the altimeter setting on the autopilot and dialed in 430 and set the altimeter.

This action was so bizarre that Abe thought Zane must be losing his mind. He remembered the radio call and answered back. "*MH370*, all right, good night."

Zane stuck a seven-inch long noiseless pistol into Abe's face and pulled the trigger. Pulling the trigger activated the crushing of a vial of prussic acid, which converted into hydrogen cyanide gas. In the dark cockpit, the action happened so fast, Abe had little time to react as he inhaled the deadly mist. *Zane was pointing his finger into his face for questioning his actions in the cockpit*, the last thought Abe had before the severe contraction of blood vessels caused his heart to stop. Abe silently slumped over the yoke, but Zane pulled him back into the seat. He positioned the body with the head back as if he were napping. He removed an aviation magazine from his book bag, and using tape with adhesive backing on both sides, he taped the open magazine over his face.

Zane lay back in his seat hyperventilating into the oxygen mask. He turned to his right. His heart was suffused with a terrible pity for the dead pilot. He remembered the mixture of emotions on his face: fear, confusion, and a kind of merciless bewilderment.

I'm sorry, Abe, he thought. *You were a better pilot than myself at 27. I'm sorry I was forced to this.*

Slowly, a little at a time, Zane raised his head. And slightly below eye-level to his left he saw the altimeter at 43,000 feet.

What the hell! How did the aircraft get in a configuration of 43,000 feet? It was the 43 seconds it took to die from the inhaled gas! He was so flustered and fixated on the murder that he set the altimeter to 430. No big deal. He could made it up with his weather radar, Doppler radar, when he was in the vicinity of the "Orca Flight," the KC-10's and F-16's. He would probably be masked in their radar when he needed to use his Doppler. They would have their transponders on, or would they, and that would aid his Doppler. An aircraft TCAS (traffic collision avoidance system) was transponder based, which was the primary reason he turned off his transponders, so other aircraft could not paint him. The old adage: aviate, navigate, and communicate popped into his head.

He turned the "Fasten Seat Belt" light on, turned off all radios, set the altimeter to 250, and dialed in the heading he memorized by running the scenario in his home simulator. There was bad weather ahead, so he made an announcement to the crew and passengers. *Safety of flight,* he thought, *Safety of flight.* The 777 could easily handle the bad weather. He did not like flying though bad weather; however, he needed to keep on the rehearsed heading and airspeed. It was fancy trigonometry along with other flight data that set him on a trajectory toward the refueling aircraft. Maybe, if it was daylight he could find the flight without using the Doppler radar. Prior to take-off, on his walk-around, he entered the avionics deck and snipped the wire leading to the antennae linking the aircraft to the Inmarsat Satellite. The same person that gave him the gas pistol told him the North Koreans would hack into the Inmarsat and, using the specific identifier code for his 777, send erroneous pings, as if flying over the Indian Ocean. North Korea acquired the hacking codes from Chinese Military hackers. They hacked into a variety of satellite programs, not just the Inmarsat. In addition, in three days, a North Korean cargo ship would drop a specially engineered black box in 18,000 feet of water in the Indian Ocean. Unlike aircraft black boxes, that are actually orange, this black box was really black.

After descending to 250, Zane accomplished six "S" Turns—all in keeping with the rehearsed rendezvous scenario he ran in his home simulator—to line-up behind the *Orca* Flight. Fifty minutes later, he was about to turn on the Doppler radar when he noticed a series of small lights, the F-16 wing-tip lights, and anti-collision strobes, in the distance below his position. In the next instant he was looking at the brilliant lighting around the tail of the KC-10, as an F-16 was mated to the KC-10 refueling boom on-loading fuel. One time, while crew-resting in Honolulu, Zane met a tanker crew and F-16 pilots. Fascinated by the art of air refueling, he talked "shop" with them for over two hours as they all got drunk. He learned about air refueling, and they learned about the triple-seven. *The information gathered in the bar proved instrumental in his nighttime rendezvous with fate, luck, destiny, or whatever,* thought Zane. He removed his oxygen mask and turned off the "Fasten Seat Belt" sign. Zane descended to 230 and maintained a position two miles in trail, directly behind the KC-10, low. He knew the other KC-10 was three miles off the nose of the tanker he trailed, with four F-16's off its left wing. *I did it! I am in the Orca Flight's radar!*

Through a camera overlooking the cockpit door a small display showed the chief purser flight attendant entering the cipher code on the door. A security feature added after 9/11. Zane watched her go through and close the door behind her.

"Peek a boo, I see you. Boy is it dark in here. Do you guys need anything? That was some awful turbulence," the thirty-six year old flight attendant said.

"Thank you, no we're fine. I apologize for the turbulence. The autopilot is acting up so we have been 'dead sticking' it. Abe did most of the flying. I don't think he ever flown much autopilot off before.

"I thought 'dead stick' flying is loss of power, not auto-pilot off. Sure tired him out. He had a bachelor party last night, or was it the night before? Anyways, what is that smell? Smells like almonds."

Zane suddenly glared at the attendant. Part of him was cold, both a physical cold and a cold in his head by what she said. *Did she know? Should I kill her? But how?* "You have a good nose. I just finished some roosted almonds. Abe ate also so we will not need a tray. Well, it should be smooth sailing the rest of the flight. The deviations to get around the weather will put us in forty minutes late. We should be on the ground in four and a half hours. How are the passengers?"

"Asleep. Not too many babies. There is twenty or so passengers from some high tech company in the states. All and all, not a bad bunch of folks."

"Great."

"Okay, just ring if you need anything."

"Thank you." He watched her leave the flight deck. Good, the people in the back probably didn't know anything was wrong—yet.

How did it come to this? Everything, he knew now, was the fault of women—too many women. Two girlfriends drove him to it all, the debts, the failed marriage, the alcohol problems, the humiliation of the sex videos, and the coming divorce. He was on the edge of an abyss, contemplating suicide, when the plan to spend time with the love of his life emerged. He had thought, he could fly the 777 into a mountain. But now there would be the mountains by the lake. His world was gone; the hijacking gave new life, new hope. The ultimate air piracy challenge, along with the training and planning, brought energy and invigoration to his depression. The women problems were reduced to one twenty-four year old Malaysian woman that he loved more than life itself. His wife and family would be well off with the insurance money. Actually, they would be better off with him dead. He would live out his remaining days with his new wife in a small villa next to a lake surrounded by mountains.

Through small binoculars, Zane watched the air refueling. For five minutes, maybe a little more, no more than that, each F-16 stayed on the boom to get his gas. *It was an amazing flying feat!* There was a rhythm to it all that Zane knew was a combination of boom operator and pilot skills. The F-16's closed in tighter off the left KC-10 wing. The fighter getting on the boom would turn off its strobe light to avoid distracting the boom operator. The four aircraft cycled through every forty-five minutes. Zane watched the last F-16 get his gas and move off the right side of the tanker, turning his strobe back on. *His anti-collision strobe and wing-tip lights! What a fool!* Zane reached up and turned them off.

After refueling his last fighter, Chief Joe Austin, KC-10 Boom Operator, stayed in the boom seat. Using his binoculars, he looked at an aircraft offset to his left behind the KC-10, about a mile and a half. Then he saw the strobe and wing-tip lights turn off. *Strangest damn thing,* Joe thought, *probably some little carrier flying to Seoul. Just because it is nautical twilight does not mean you turn your lights off. Stupid pilot! Probably some kid flying the jet.* Then he watched the plane take a hard right bank, which was actually a left because Joe was looking backwards. Joe noticed the tail logo. He drew a little picture in his checklist of the logo. *I'll have to look that up some time. Hell, it looked like a triple-seven.*

Chapter 10

North Korea

March 9, 2014, 0830 hours

The jet turned ninety-degrees left away from the Sea of Japan toward its rendezvous with the Democratic People's Republic of Korea. Zane set the aircraft on a descent for a VFR (visual flight rules) landing at Pyongyang. In the mission profile in his simulator, he loaded the land features from Google Maps and was confident he could locate such a large city next to a prominent river without using radios and navigation aids from the FMC (Flight Management Computer). The sun was behind him and the visibility excellent.

Out of nowhere two fighter jets appeared off the left. At first, Zane thought they were U.S. F-15's but seconds later knew they were MIG-29's. One jet rocked his wings and the pilot made a downward pointing gesture with his finger. The two pilots were told bluntly, "You will be executed by firing squad if the jet does not land at Hwangsuwon Airport!" Without radio contact, the aggressive proximity of the MIG-29's to the triple seven sent a clear message--descend now! The maxim drilled into a pilot to lose altitude went: gear, flaps, and slats. One MIG-29 pulled ahead of the 777 in a gesture that said, follow me, while the other MIG maintained a position off the triple-seven's left wing. Zane saw the airfield in a valley surrounded by mountains. Due to the configuration he was in with relation to altitude and distance from the airfield, Zane put the aircraft into a corkscrew nose-dive. The fighters careened around him, the air crackling in thunder. Zane focused landing the jet "on the numbers" on the runway and flaring the jet.

On the ground, following a truck, in a heartbeat, all was a nightmare. It was an eerie feeling and Zane thought, *I just made a BIG mistake!* Zane heard the commotion from the passengers. The chief purser entered the cockpit yelling questions. She noticed the dead co-pilot and slammed her fist on Zane, then the other, then the first once more; Abe was slumped on the yoke, the aircraft connected to a tug and towed into a large hangar to avoid the thrice-weekly passes by a U.S. spy satellite. A sophisticated airliner and part of modern technology, had been hijacked by one man swimming in his emotions—not just swimming but drowning.

The entry door was opened from the outside by the EMERGENCY lever that activated a pneumatic bottle, blowing the door open in seconds. Experts in the art of execution and torture, Camp 14 Guards, were the first to enter the jet, followed by the mastermind of the hijacking, Chul moo. He required the guards carry out orders exactly and be impervious to suffering. Their orders: put the passengers on two buses, with bared windows, and drive to Office 35 at Camp 14—and that is what they did. It was nothing out of the ordinary, people were rounded up all the time and bused to labor camps. The Nazis, too, operated in the same manner seventy years ago.

Chul moo entered the flight station and Zane saw him approaching with a knife. *Was there any way to slow him down?* Using a Karambit knife, he sliced Zane's neck from ear to ear. Because of his rise in the party, he had not killed in years and he missed it. *Murder,* Chul moo thought, *he liked killing people.*

Monday morning, March 17, 2014, Chul moo sat in the back seat of a black Mercedes Stretch as the car pulled through the gate of the Ryongsong Residence. Three days prior, Chul moo had learned that a rumor was spread in the morning, prior to a Supreme People's Assembly (SPA) meeting, that North Korea was involved in the hijacking of the missing Boeing 777 aircraft. Four people were taken into a public square and shot. Kim Jong un presided at the SPA gathering and the entire assemblage remained bowed low at the waist for close to five minutes before the meeting started. An action that had not occurred since Kim Il sung chaired the assembly in 1987. Kim Jong un made the announcement that the economy warranted a fifteen percent pay raise for SPA and WPK (worker's party of Korea) Central Committee members.

"Brilliant Comrade?" Chul moo stuck his head through the door to find Kim Jong un looking over counterfeit hundred dollar bills.

"Yes, yes," Jong Un responded, looking up. "How did you do it? They are beautiful. An absolutely perfect match with a note printed in Washington. It is on this great achievement that I ordered a pay raise!"

"I apologize for the delay, brilliant comrade," Chul moo said, his head bowed at the waist. He remained bowed till Jong un spoke.

"Nonsense, Chul moo, it only took six months to crack the blue '3D security ribbon' and other features on the newly released bill. How? How did you do it?"

"Well, let me just say I offered a deal they (Office 39 counterfeit division) couldn't refuse," Chul moo answered.

Kim Jong un looked out the large window, imported from Austria, at the large courtyard nestled in the Pines. *Where have I heard that? Oh, yes, it was a Godfather movie.* He felt like Michael Corleone after he killed all his enemies and became the Godfather. He turned to Chul moo. "What happened to the pilot?"

"I killed him."

"The plane?"

"It has been chopped up and put into an incinerator, brilliant comrade," he answered. "I supervised the destruction myself."

"The team? Where are they?"

"Our agents are in Düsseldorf, Germany. I added a female agent from the 'seed-bearing' program. It is an operation only myself, you, and Putin know about. I will fill you in as the operation progresses. The code name is *Alps*. Supreme Leader, this operation pales in comparison to our Great Hijacking," Chul moo replied stonily.

Kim Jong un nodded, then looked back out the window. He remembered a quote from *Moby Dick*. But now he changed the quote, *as long as there are men, ships, planes, and seas, there will be mysteries.* Yes, that is what I will say if ever questioned about the hijacking. He turned around and looked at Chul moo. "The passengers, where are the passengers?"

"Camp 14."

Chapter 11

Luke

May 3, 2014

Sam Young could only remember one time upon when he actually shot better than his adopted father, Luke Young. It was when he was twelve and it was with a BB gun prior to the New York State BB gun finals. Looking back at it now with murky thoughts as Sam entered his fifth decade, he may not have outscored his dad. His father probably let him win to booster his confidence going into the final shooting match. There may have been another occasion, but if so Sam did not remember it.

It was a wet, dreary afternoon and the Canadian Geese could be heard all around them. Sam stood behind his father, holding the binoculars but not looking through them, watching silently as his father, in the kneeling position, prepared to shoot coke cans five hundred yards away. He watched a mosquito feast on the side of his Father's neck. Throughout his kneeling, Luke didn't move a muscle. He just maintained his shooting position, his attention absolutely focused down the PU sniper scope secured to the top of the 91/30 Mosin-Nagant rifle. At age sixty-seven, Luke was aware of every aspect of the environment that could affect his shots. He watched the crosshairs bent with his pulse and slowly, gently squeezed the trigger. The explosion was deafening, mixed with the beating wings of thousands of geese taking off, and the working of the bolt on the rifle as Luke emptied the five-round clip. But Sam never saw the shattered coke cans or heard the geese, it was the memory of vision flashes, and something stirred deep within Sam. It reached back through the years—all the killings that Chul moo must have committed—and ended thinking of his father. Luke forged Sam's character and made him into what he ultimately became—an Air Force Pararescuemen. Pararescue, the powerful model that laid the foundation for Sam's life. Luke, without trying, steered Sam in a direction that led to his destiny.

Finally, Luke eased up from the kneeling position, turned and very carefully slapped the mosquito on his neck. He wiped the blood on his pant leg. He looked at Sam, who attempted to help him up, and he said, "How did I do?" He knew the shooting was extraordinary.

Sam smiled. "You are getting better with age, dad," Sam said, but his smile held confusion. "What kind of rifle is that?"

"This is a 91/30 Mosin-Nagant, a Russian sniper rifle. It was used in the Battle of Stalingrad. The longest continuously serving firearm in history," Luke said dryly, handing the rifle to Sam.

"It is heavy, too heavy and long to secure with the belly band of a parachute harness. Where did you get it?"

"Mike gave it to me."

"Mike Perry?"

For a while Luke stood looking toward the coke cans and listened to the sounds of the geese, the squawking and squawking—and he didn't hear his son asking the question again. "I am going to go on a tour to North Korea. One of those old folks tours arranged around a basketball exhibition game. I always enjoyed watching Red Robin when he played for the NBA. He is playing in an exhibition game for that new leader . . . . what is his name?"

"Kim Jong un," Sam said.

Luke could see the wheels turning in Sam's head as he absorbed what the older man had said.

Chapter 12

The Diplomat

June 2, 2014

CIA Director Mike Perry followed Chul moo's rise in power within the Kim regime for close to thirty years. On Seoraksan Mountain in 1984, when Chul moo, a Special Forces captain in the People's Army, killed two men in Mike's army reserve unit, Mike vowed to himself, a commitment, to make Chul moo answer for his crime. His men killed by one bullet from a sniper rifle. In 1994, when Kim Il sung proclaimed Chul Moo as his long lost son, state media glorified the killing of two American imperialist by Chul moo. He became a 'legend' and gave needed boost to the Kim cult. Mike, however, knew his identity, the closely guarded secret of his birth and twin brother, and if what he had pieced together was accurate, that same man, that 'legend' was no great hero but instead a sick psychopathic killer. He was believed responsible for the death of Sam Young's step-mother, the deaths of three Canadians in a car bombing in Niagara Falls, the death of a Russian FSB Agent in Canada, and the death of a female North Korean agent in South Korea. Mike knew the deaths caused by Chul moo, the monster, were merely the tip of the iceberg. He reclined in his executive chair, pushed a few buttons on a remote, and a sliding panel on the wall opened, revealing a 52 inch flat screen TV. He watched Chul moo on CNN dressed in a suit, stroll into the United Nations in New York. His hair was an iron-gray while Mike's was nearly bald. Not only was he in charge of Office 35 & 39, but he was a North Korean diplomat involved in talks over North Korean nuclear weapons. He was believed by some in his agency as an heir to the Presidency in the event of Kim Jong un's death. Mike found it repulsive that a thug like Chul moo had freedom of movement.

Mike's intuition, along with the professional in him, was telling him he was nearing the end of a long journey. Mike was a Second Lieutenant, Intelligence Officer, stationed at Panmunjom near the DMZ in 1976 when the "Tree Cutting Incident" took place. Mike's homosexual lover was Army Captain Terry Reid, assigned to the Military Police Detachment. Their relationship was a closely guarded secret. They had dreams of traveling the world together while assigned to various army postings throughout the world. On August 18, 1976, Terry was supervising a work detail in the Demilitarized Zone when a North Korean soldier murdered him with an axe. From that day forward, Mike Perry dedicated his life toward hitting at the North Korean regime. He became the Army's intelligence expert on Korea and this landed him a job with the DIA, where he was the lead analyst concerning the Korean peninsula. He joined a Special Forces Reserve Detachment out of Fort Belvoir near Washington DC. The unit's area of responsibility was Asia, with an emphasis on Korea. Mike enjoyed the reserve because of the contrast from his desk job. The Army Reserve offered the opportunity of travel on military orders to Korea at any given time. His TDYs to Korea as a reservist strengthened his relationship with TJ Hill, an Air Force Pararescuemen stationed at Osan Air Base.

Chul moo did not know of the vendetta the DCIA had for him. Mike never came close enough to Chul moo for him to know that. . . . But Mike knew what he was, what he would do to him, and how Chul moo played into a grand plan involving the hermit kingdom of Korea. The egg was laid by CIA Director Casey, Mike nurtured it, and waited for the day to hatch it. So he was careful.

At seven fifteen on a warm Sunday night, the door to the DCIA's office opened and retired Modesto Detective Dodge Hender stepped through. He walked briskly toward the desk, his arm extended to shake Mike's hand.

"Good to see you Dodge. But it is not fair. How do you do it?" Mike asked.

"Sir?"

"You have not aged a bit! You still have a full head of hair. And call me Mike. How long has it been? Twenty years?" He looked at Dodge with mild curiosity. "What's the secret?"

"Well, a cop's safety retirement allowed me to retire at age fifty-five with a damn near full pension. My boys are out of the house. Happy wife, happy life," Dodge said while looking around the office at the walls lined with monitors and other electronic gear whose nature was not immediately apparent. "You can't get out of the game Mike. I commend you. You made it to the top."

"Dodge, I want out of the game," he lied, thinking about a new threat to national security, an organization calling themselves ISIS, short for Islamic State of Iraq and Syria. "There is one final task I want to put a closure on."

Dodge didn't have to be a mindreader to know the task he mentioned: the task Mike assigned to him twenty years ago when he was an analyst or pencil pusher in the agency. The task of investigating the murder of Sam Young's step-mother.

"It's Chul moo. That's what we need to talk about, Dodge. I appreciate you holding the file after concluding your investigation. I trust you more than I trust the agencies around me. How long has it been?"

"Eight years, sir. Here is the file." Dodge pushed the brown folder across the desk toward the DCI.

Not looking at the folder, but keeping his eyes fixed on the retired Modesto Detective, Mike spoke, "Okay, I forget. Give me a synopsis of your investigation."

For Dodge, every detail of his investigation was fresh to him, not tarnished by time. He had waited for this moment for years. He didn't believe that Mike forgot the details. That is what he wanted him to believe: the top spy already knew everything in the report, and more. Years ago, Dodge thought up all sorts of unexpected directions the information from his investigation would go. Now he no longer was concerned or considered the outcome, but he knew Mike had his own agenda, his own reasons for asking for the file. Closure would come soon.

"Through DNA, Chul moo can be linked to the murder of Senior Master Sergeant Donald Albright in 1984, Sam Young's step-mother in 94, and to a stay in an IRA safe house along Lake Ontario after the murder, which links him to the 'Rainbow Bridge car bombing' when three people were killed. He cut himself with the kitchen knife he used in the Albright murder. There was two blood types on Don's flight suit: one being his own and the second I was not sure. I ran the DNA through the DNA databank known as the Combined DNA Indez System (CODIS) and came up with a firm match," Dodge said crisply.

"The match was Sam Young," the DCI interrupted him in a low, harsh voice barely recognizable.

"Exactly. I investigated Sam Young and determined it was impossible for him to commit the murder. He was at Little River Naval Base preparing for a classified extraction mission. I remember our conversation at Luke Young's house and how you pretty much determined Chul moo was the killer. I never for a minute believed Sam was the killer, despite the hard DNA evidence."

"You then interviewed Luke Young and learned about Sam's background, the adoption, and his twin brother Chul moo."

"Well, yes and no, it was helpful talking to Luke but new DNA techniques, particularly PCR (Polymerase Chain Reaction) and STR (Short Tandem Repeat) established Chul moo's DNA, along with his fingerprints, from a bottle of beer he drank at the IRA safe house along the lake. In addition, I obtained a hair follicle from a reclining chair. But the damning evidence was the fingerprints and DNA trail he left in the boat house when he made the car bomb. It is all firm evidence of time and place linking him to the murder and car bombing. I am sure the Canadians may be interested in this information."

"The Canadians are interested," he told Dodge, avoiding his unrelenting gaze. "They link Chul moo to the murder of the 'man with no eyes.' Are you familiar with that murder?"

"Yes, that murder made me realize the espionage/global aspect of this whole ordeal. All the connections and dots too complicated for a city homicide detective. And why me? Why not the FBI or some secret squirrel organization?"

"Dodge, like I told you before, I can trust you more than big agencies fighting turf battles and power trips. Have you ever discussed this investigation with anyone?" Mike was reminding Dodge of the requirement placed on him at Luke Young's house.

"No one. Just you from time to time. What now?"

Dodge watched the director remove a bottle of Scotch and two glasses from his desk. He poured in the two glasses. "I don't know how to thank you, Dodge," Mike began. "Thank you, it is over for you. Salute!"

Dodge was sitting to attention, holding his Scotch glass in front of him with both hands, as if someone had handed it to him as a reward.

"I can assure you it is not over for Chul Moo but it will soon be over for him."

An hour after his meeting, on the way to Dulles Airport, under the black night sky, on Highway 66, just outside of Falls Church, the headlights from the car in front of Dodge Hender began to blur. By the time he finished rubbing his eyes, he was dead. The rental car he was driving veered off the highway and flipped when it hit an embankment.

The Falls Church Police accident investigation revealed the fifty-seven year old retired Homicide Detective died from a heart attack.

Chapter 13

Kuala Lumpur

July 7, 2014

Chen was prone to see an omen when Mike Perry asked him if he would go to Kuala Lumpur to investigate why so many 'supernotes' were showing up around the city. He didn't believe in black cats under ladders, mirrors shattering by reflections, or two-headed snakes—none of these things will rattle him. He did believe in déjà vu, that events tend to repeat themselves, or at least rhythm. He was partnered up with Don Albright, the wiz kid, as Chen often called him, an ex-Japanese Pararescuemen turned CIRO (Cabinet Intelligence and Research) agent. His mother, the Deputy Director of CIRO, linked the bar Kimmy's in Subang Jaya to smuggling counterfeit Yen inside of pirated DVDs. CIRO traced the Yen to North Korea.

The two walked along a narrow side alley off of Petaling Street, the night market Chinatown of Kuala Lumpur. The vendor stalls selling everything from Hello Kitty watches, pirated DVDs, fake Rolex watches, and fried chicken. The air was dense with humidity and smells of fried grasshoppers and fish, beer, the hum of conversation and laughter, and the beeping of tri-pod motorcycle taxis fighting their way through pockets of pedestrians. The buildings were low, made of wood, but the high-rise structures of a modern city loomed overhead in the distance. Mixed in among the vending stalls were bars with illuminated signs running up the sides, advertising go-go girls and dancers. The alley was crowded with foreigners out for a deal on a cheap Rolex or pirated DVD, couples walking arm on arm on their way to dinner, and the street prostitutes. The tourist gawking at the spectacle. After moving through the crowds, Chen saw a sign for Kimmy's, a two-story building squeezed in-between vending stalls.

They went up the stairs to the bar, bathed in dim green lights, and meandered through the tourist, finding seats along the side. Chen trusted the Japanese intelligence as he scanned the bar that soon became standing room only, for a clue, something out of the ordinary. Alarm bells, a little thing called instinct, began to sound in Chen's head.

He became hyped, the bar stood out with clarity, and he cued in on an Asian woman at the bar. She fell into his Déjà vu thoughts. He thought he was having a terrible confused dream—blood, broken ribs, the smell of expensive perfume—while watching her. The woman was an exact look-alike of Zoey, a transgender, involved in money laundering with the Chinese Triad. Chen's hairless chest covered with Goosebumps as he remembered snapping Zoey's neck in a full-nelson wrestling move some fourteen years earlier. Zoey tried to shoot him in a parking garage elevator and that started the fight for his life. The bullet ripped part of his left earlobe off, almost hitting him in the head.

Chen asked Don Albright, if he saw her, and Don nodded. Chen not taking his eyes off the entrance, which reminded him of the entrance to the Golden Dragon Restaurant in San Francisco. This sent Chen back in time. *Close to forty years ago, he was a Wah Ching gang member and involved in the "Golden Dragon" shootout. Chen escaped the police, went into hiding, and joined the Air Force. He became an Air Force Pararescuemen or PJ, met a PJ named Sam Young, and went on a mission with him in South Korea that ended in North Korea, married Sam's sister, and joined the Federal Reserve in San Francisco. That was the short version of his "roller coaster" life.* Chen snapped out of his reverie, attributing the Asian at the bar and the entrance to *ennui,* the ghost of his past, but said nothing to Don. Speech all at once seemed hard; he felt a debilitating force grip him, something feverish and constant, like a low-grade flu.

At last, Chen opened Microsoft Office 365 on his encrypted and supposedly unjammable, unhackable cell phone. The phone had unique encryption keys, known only by Chen, along with the ability to encrypt calls and text—as well as enable private web browsing and cloud storage. He scrolled through various word documents until he came to the "Zoey" file.

"It's him!" Chen almost shouted. Then, in a lower tone of voice: "That is Zoey's identical twin brother. There can be no doubt. I am sure he is dangerous . . . . I want you to send your folks a massage and ask for an inquiry on Auwut Shinawatra, a Thai citizen." Chen showed his cell phone to Don. Don typed the message, in Japanese encryption keys known only by himself and his mother, in his DoCoMo phone and clicked the SEND button.

"Give CIRO a few minutes. Our computer nerds are the best."

"I know."

"The she is a he?" Don asked. "I remember Zoey from some files my mother had me read. You killed Zoey. Snapped his neck in a parking garage in Frisco if I remember right."

Chen looked at him, one eyebrow raised. "You are sharp like your father."

"You think so?" Don wore the expression of a man hearing something too good to be true. He never knew his father. His mother was pregnant with him when Chul moo Kim killed his father in Sacramento.

Chen knew Don liked hearing about his father. "Fast rope. I'm sure you know about fast rope."

"Sure, I've done it many times. It has to be the fastest way of getting out of a hovering helicopter. The navy SEALs fasted roped into bin Laden's compound out of HH-60, Blackhawks."

"Well your father invented fast rope."

"Is that right. Tell me about it."

"When your dad went through PJ School at Lackland AFB, or OL-J, as we called it, which was short for Operating Location J, PJ students carried this big, thick rope around everywhere they went. Actually, they ran in-step with the rope. Brass couplings were attached to each end of the rope. You could never touch the brass ends. It was so shiny you could shave in it. If the PJs went inside a building, they coiled the rope in an A-3 bag and took the rope with them."

Don only sat, looking at Chen and soaking up every word.

Chen sighed, then continued with the story. "Years later, we were flying SOLL (special ops low-level) missions in 53's out of McClellan AFB. Your dad started talking about the rope used at PJ School. He ordered a similar rope and devised a way of hooking it up to the hoist on the HH-53. He ran all the paperwork through the Wing and up to Headquarters for test and evaluation. So the PJs at McClellan began fast roping out of Jolly Greens, the HH-53s. Now the Sacramento Sheriff's Department had a small helicopter in a hangar next to the PJ Section. They saw what we were doing and took the idea to some SWAT (special weapons assault team) convention. The next thing you know military and police agencies all around the world are fast roping."

Don's phone made a small beep as the inquiry came back. "Let's see what we got." Don read the Japanese characters, thankfully seeing them clearly under the bar's green lights. "Chen, this is interesting."

"Talk to me, brother. Tell me whatever you've got---"

"He goes by the name Sylvia, runs a business called 'Cold Weapons,' an online store selling knives, swords, and daggers, and is suspected of belonging to the Chinese Triad."

"Don?" said Chen, cutting him off. "I bet one of the largest clients is the Russian Defense Minister. Am I right?"

"Funny you ask. I was just getting to that. It appears the largest buyer is Russian Defense Minister Shoygu. You will never guess who another buyer is. . ." Don's voice dropped to a painful whisper.

"Chul moo Kim in North Korea! And on paper, anyways, many of the replica weapons are produced and shipped from North Korea."

"Exactly. There is a large shipment of weapons that will depart KL tomorrow destined for Russia. Which explains Sylvia's presence. How did you know about the Defense Minister?"

"Shoygu is Putin's right hand man, the architect of the annexation of Crimea. He happens to have one of the largest, most valuable collection of cold weapons. There is a money trail that branches world-wide, but ultimately lead back to two men—Vladimir Putin and Kim Jong un." Chen paused. "The vast criminal empire of the two mafia – based organized state businesses."

"Hey, it looks like the computer nerds were able to acquire the hotel Sylvia is staying at through his credit card. Stand-by they are searching for the location," Don said, surprised, as he used his fingers to expand the Japanese characters on the phone.

Chen surmised Sylvia would take the tall Dane man back to his hotel for sex soon . . . if his hotel was within walking distance, and Chen's instinct told him the hotel was close.

"BINGO! He is staying in a dive motel just a few blocks from here."

Chen turned, looked at the exit, then looked at Don. "Send a message to get the 'ball rolling' for a possible emergency extraction out of KL," he said.

A plan cohered. It was improvised, it was dangerous, but given the parameters, Chen thought it would work.

The motel, Anton Inn, was located in a small alley away from the main traffic of Chinatown. In violation of local fire ordinances, the alley was used primarily for storage. Chen and Don hung in the shadow inside the alley behind laundry carts and maintained a good view, awaiting their prey. Don snipped the electrical lines leading to three overhead lights. This reduced the opportunity of someone seeing their face. What light there was came from an inadequate sodium vapor light a few hundred yards away. Chen heard girlish laughter. Sylvia arrived with the tall man at 0130 hours. Don noted the time. He saw Sylvia look around before stopping. The two were out of hearing range from Don and Chen; however, Don wore a state-of-the-art Digital Hearing Aid in his left ear. A branch of the Japanese Defense Intelligence (JDI) called Research and Development engineered the spy craft for CIRO. The research branch worked with contractors in the private sector. To recruit contractors in the private sector, JDI appealed to the company owner's patriotism and personal history. The majority of Japanese CEO's were veterans of World War Two or children of war heroes. In conjunction with Don's computer watch that linked to his cell phone, the conversation was up-linked via satellite in real time to CIRO in Japan.

Drunk and laughing, Sylvia paused when he was in the shadow. "A second airline incident with the same airline may be in the plan," a voice that was not Sylvia's said.

With his left ear pointed at the two, Don enjoyed crystal clear, natural sound without suffering any annoying background noise. He thought the broken English spoken came from a Russian, not a Dane. Classic Russian, masked by a few years living in Great Britain.

"I think it is a mistake, but what difference does it make what I think. I was paid with 'PBFs' for helping 'honey trap' that horny pilot."

"We have a problem," the Russian said.

Sylvia gave the Russian a sharp look. "What is the problem?"

"You are connected with MH370," he said.

Sylvia looked intently at his friend, who had been his lover over the past two years. Then he lowered his eyes.

The Russian attempted to throw a punch at Sylvia. Sylvia blocked it instinctively and at the same time removed a curved blade from his belt buckle. With one quick, fluid motion, Sylvia sliced across the Russian's carotid artery. The Russian fell backwards, clutching his neck in an attempt to stop the bleeding. He dropped to the ground.

Sylvia felt an ice-cold shiver run down his back. He spun around, away from the fallen Russian, and toward a noise he heard from the carts. Slowly he turned and looked around but there was no-one.

"Hello, Zoey's brother," came a low voice from somewhere in front of him.

Sylvia saw Chen and Don's figure materialize next to the laundry cart.

"You killed my brother," Sylvia said in a neutral tone. "Now you want to kill me."

Quick as lightning, Sylvia dropped into a Hapkido low spin kick, dropping Chen and at the same time rising and continuing into a full spin kick delivered to Don's head. Out of the corner of his eye he saw the two recover and mount an attack. He pulled a laundry cart toward the two, using all the strength in his arms.

They saw the laundry cart coming and threw themselves to one side. A corner of the cart struck Don on the shoulder, but he was not phased. Chen's head appeared from the side of the cart when Sylvia slashed the buckle blade at him. The blade took off a piece of Chen's right ear. He grunted and managed to grab the arm with the blade but sustained a knee to the groin, along with a head-butt while holding the arm. Don lunged a body blow below Sylvia's knees as he grabbed both legs, taking Sylvia down to the pavement.

Chen was thinking hard. He had lost a piece of his ear, but thanks to Don, Sylvia was now subdued on the pavement by the two of them. He removed the blade by snapping the wrist, breaking bones that connected the hand to the arm. Chen pressed the blade to Sylvia's throat, cutting the skin next to the carotid artery.

Weeping, holding his broken hand to his chest, and scared by the blade to his throat, Sylvia did not move. He sprawled on his back on the pavement with Don on top of his legs. Sylvia felt pain, despair, and wretched fear. The fear was by far the worst, and he decided to take a risk.

"I want to know about MH370 and the honey trap," Don asked from his position below Sylvia's waist.

"Fuck you!" Sylvia whispered, but Chen heard. He saw the cricoid cartilage, a soft spot just below the Adam's Apple. He pressed the blade into the cricoid cartilage, which could kill Sylvia quickly. The exact spot where a cricothyroidotomy is performed, if the life-saving procedure is warranted. Chen had cut a cricoid before, not on a man but on a goat in Pararescue medical training. A goat's cricoid cartilage is similar to a human's; therefore, he knew how far he could cut without severing the cartilage. Chen, moving with a finicky, surgical precision, began cutting the cricoid cartilage.

Sylvia made low, in-the-throat sobs. This seemed to satisfy Chen; he stopped the incision. He looked at Sylvia. His face was chalky white, and his eyes, though open, seemed dull and lifeless.

"Koreans hijacked the jet. Flew it to North Korea," Sylvia blubbered.

"How? I want details," Chen said without expression, as if he were a poker-player in a high-stakes game. He pressed the blade against the cartilage.

"Myself and a Korean that called herself Lily sex played a pilot named Zane into flying the jet to North Korea. The Koreans did something with computers and hacking to fool everyone into thinking the plane crashed in the Indian Ocean."

Chen nodded matter-of-factly. He removed the blade from the neck.

"The man you killed mentioned another airliner. Who is he and what does it mean? Where is Lily?" Don asked. "And I want the name of the ship with the weapons shipment that leaves tomorrow."

"He is Russian. I don't really know how, but they are caught into the mess. They are planning on shooting down a Malaysian Airlines jet to distract attention from Ukraine, I think—Putin's plan. Lily went to Europe, France or Germany," Sylvia's lips twitched in a smile. "*Green Dog*! The *Green Dog* is the ship." He managed to bring his good arm down to his side and removed a miniature ice pick from the same belt that hid the other blade. He gave Chen a quick gleaming look before he tried to plunge the pick into Chen's ribs.

Sylvia's gleam gave away his intention. Chen grabbed Sylvia's wrist and redirected the pick into the incision over the cricoid cartilage. The pick punctured through the cartilage and made another hole on the opposite side. Sylvia fixed Chen with his eyes. Tiny, fierce eyes of a dying man. In his desperation he reached to Chen but then clutched his own neck. There was a wheezing, sucking sound mixed with the blood. He died, literally breath by breath. Chen drew no pleasure from killing, as blood gushed over his hands and arms. Amazingly, Sylvia's heart still pumped blood, but soon it stopped.

Kneeling in the shadows above the bodies, Don took two pictures with his cell phone. The special lens in his phone was capable of capturing images in complete darkness. It was as simple as point and shoot. Next, he opened a fingerprint app on his cell and quickly took complete fingerprints of the two. While Don took the fingerprints, Chen found their wallets and removed the money. Chen thought the hundred dollar bills were authentic just by the feel and quick glance. He arranged their identifications on the pavement so Don could get a picture. Chen threw the wallets next to the bodies. The police would suspect they were murdered for money. After a quick glance of the crime scene they departed. They looked around the alley, turning in a complete circle. Nobody; no witnesses. They moved into the crowded streets and for the time being, at least, they felt alone among the crowd.

Akio Inoue, a Japanese Consulate Officer, awoke by the sound of a "barking dog" ringtone on his cell phone. Tokyo issued an encrypted order at one-thirty in the morning. He was to locate two men in the Chinatown bar district and take them north, up the coast. Tsukuba Space Center tracked one of the men by his cell phone and constantly knew his exact location. Akio would be vectored to his location and use the password "can you swim?" to ID the man. He never received such "off-the-wall" orders and became excited that this may be "spook" type work. He always dreamed of intelligence work instead of his hum drum embassy administration job. His fantasies may become reality, and he knew this, perhaps, was a test that he must complete without failure.

It was three o'clock in the morning in Chinatown, the brightly lit Petaling street surrounded by bars and restaurants, deserted except for prostitutes, gang members, and some tourist; most were drunk, several elated, most looking to made money. Akio weaved his way down the street in a 1964 Chang Jiang, CJ750, motorcycle with a one-wheeled side car attached to the bike. The side car was yellow with a large Pokemon decal on the front. Wearing shorts, a yellow tank top, yellow sneakers, and a yellow Pokemon cap, Akio appeared to belong to the night-life of Chinatown. He taped his cell phone between the handle bars so he could view a street map with his "target fix." He scanned the street while glancing at his cell phone, awestruck by the haven of girls in mini-skirts. A purple light enveloped Chinatown, and a sense that the night action was winding down lessened the traffic. Yet, the CJ750 dodged among the bicycles, taxi cabs, and pedestrians with the skill that came from maneuvering through Tokyo's traffic.

BEEP-BEEP-BEEP!

The beeping horn had finally gotten Chen and Don's full attention, and they stopped and moved to the side of the street so the crazy kid on the bike could pass. Akio shut the motorcycle off as it glided next to his "target fix."

"Can you swim?" Akio asked Don in Japanese.

"Like a fish," Don replied. He wore the expression of a man seeing something too good to be true as the two of them climbed in the side car. Seconds later, the motorcycle moved down Pedaling Street, away from Chinatown.

Akio felt an enormous relief as he departed with the two men in the side car. An ear-shattering siren erupted, so loud that everyone on the street stepped back as a police car with flashing lights sped through the street. Akio wandered if it had anything to do with his new occupants. But he didn't want to think about those things, didn't care about those things. What he cared about was getting the two out of his motorcycle, off his hands, and delivered to a man changing a tire, next to a red jeep with flashing green lights.

Akio blinked his eyes, annoyed by the flashing lights ahead of him, brighter as he drove closer. Slowly, he drove off the road, next to a large Japanese man holding a tire iron, and killed the engine. Chen and Don stepped out of the side car. The man nodded to Akio and waved his hand, a gesture along with his gaze clearly indicated to Akio his job was over.

"Give me your hotel keys and passports," he said to both of them. "I will handle clearing you out of the country."

Chen and Don handed their passports and electronic room cards to the man. "I am in room 301 at Traders Hotel," Chen said.

"And I am in the room across his, room 328," replied Don simply.

A cell phone rang. The man answered it. "Hai." He listened for ten seconds and then hung up. "No time to waste," he said. "A highway patrol unit will be here in 8-10 minutes. Here are two surf boards along with swim paddles for your hands. Paddle out two miles for your pick-up." He studied their faces, his narrow, slit-eyes roving, boring into theirs.

Don nodded his head to say, yes, picked up the surf board and paddles and gave Chen a smile as he headed for the ocean.

"Into the ocean?" asked Chen.

"Yes."

"Thanks," Chen replied calmly, grabbing the board, paddles, and water-proof backpack. Since Chen just managed to kill a man on foreign soil and the thought of Malaysian Prison frightened him, he savored the security of the open ocean. The semi-commando duo paddled out to sea. Suddenly, the flashing green lights extinguished.

The *Jinryu*, SS-507, Soryu-class submarine, surfaced directly in front of the two "surfers." Japanese Defense Forces changed the naming convention with the Soryu-class submarines and began naming the vessels after mythological creatures. The *Jinryu*, the most advanced non-nuclear submarine in the world, was the god dragon. China's rising military received most press coverage concerning Asia's militaries. However, it was Japan's Self-Defense Forces that could pack quite a punch, not the Chinese Military. Particularly the Soryu-class submarines. Japan had operated submarines for many decades, yet the Chinese did not even have anti-submarine warfare (ASW) capabilities. *You could always trust the Japanese to be punctual*, Chen thought. He smiled as a small RPA (remotely powered aircraft) landed on the submarine deck. The crewmen were kind and pulled the two onto the sub deck with a rope. The *Jinryu* submerged.

Don and Chen spent a few minutes changing into dry clothes before the *Jinryu* commander contacted them. "So good of you to drop by," said Commander Kazuki Kano, shaking hands and bowing. Kano, a second-generation submariner, an officer trained at Naval Academy Etajima. His father, a World War II Japanese submariner, survived the war and lived into old age, a rare occurrence in Japanese Naval History. Kano spent most of his life underwater in the seas surrounding Japan. He was a major presence in a submarine.

Traditionally Japanese submarines operated in the Tsugaru Strait, Tsushima Strait, Kanmon Strait, and the Soya Strait. Lately, Japan took on a more China-centric deployment plan, especially with the Senkakus and Ryukyu Islands in mind. In addition, piracy presented a growing problem in the Malacca Strait, a sea corridor that 80% of

Japan's oil passed through. Piracy was extremely hard to stop. When the pressure against it grows too great, it just shifts locations.

"Permission to board ship, sir," Chen asked. He remembered someone telling him that foreign military must receive permission from the ship's skipper when boarding their vessel.

"Permission granted, but I kindly ask you tell no one that a Japanese submarine was involved in your extraction." The *Jinryu* was operating in the Malacca Strait and no one knew of its presence, not even the U.S. Pacific Fleet that had submarines in the same waters. Kano wanted to keep *Jinryu's* location secret.

"You have my word, sir," Chen said, snapping to attention and saluting.

There followed a few seconds of silence. Then: "Very well. You two will be with us for a few days. Another operation, your transfer to another ship is being coordinated. Make yourself at home. Is there anything you need?"

"A magnifying glass. Can you get me a magnifying glass?" Chen asked.

Kano was smart and professional enough to spot that Chen was a military commando in some capacity, despite his older age. The request had surprising impact, as Kano watched him, and obviously Chen needed to attend to a matter that required meticulous detail. Kano made a mental note to have lunch with Don's mother sometime soon. She ran CIRO well, and he had some ideas on covert operations.

In the small birth area over a small plastic desk, Chen adjusted the magnifying glass over one of Sylvia's hundred dollar bills, the eyes behind the glass hawk-like, acutely suspicious of what he surveyed. What was unusual, however, was the fact that he was looking at a real "Ben Franklin." He could not believe it. *It must be clean money, laundered from "supernotes."* Sylvia's words, *"paid in PBFs,"* that Don told him kept popping into his head. *PBFs? What is a PBF?*

Chen laughed, his flat eyes close to shining—*Perfect Ben Franklin!* He returned to examination of the note. After thirty minutes, he discovered a small, slight mark by the

3-D Security Ribbon that did not belong on a Bureau of Engraving and Printing note. For a minute, while inspecting the note, Chen could hardly breathe. It was as though he were suffocating. He checked Sylvia's other bills by tilting the notes back and forth while focusing on the blue ribbon—same mark in all of them. Over a decade of research and development went into the new security features, particularly the 3-D Security Ribbon and the color-shifting bell, and the North Koreans reverse-engineered the note to perfection.

"Don!" Chen whispered in a shout. "We have another mission!"

"Mission?" he asked

"The *Green Dog*. We are going to conduct a night boarding and take a look around," he said. His teeth were clamped together from the pain of his cut ear, and the words came out sounding squeezed. "If it's the ship I think it is, let me just say I already know my way around." *I can't believe they never changed the name of the ship*, Chen thought.

Chapter 14

"Black Plastic"

July 9th, 2014

The level of risk increased considerably for ships that routinely transited hostile waters after September 11th. The *Green Dog*, a Chinese Containership, was in the Malacca Strait, one of the busiest waterways in the world, and prime hunting grounds for pirates. The deck of the *Green Dog* was flooded in bright light, like Times Square on New Year's Eve, as the ship traveled a course south toward Singapore; fire hoses shot water out into the darkness. This was all part of the antipiracy defenses. A hundred years ago, ships often spread carpet nails on the deck at night as their antipiracy weapon.

As the Captain of the *Green Dog* looked out and down at the towering clutter of bright lights, it dawned on him how the measures were more for show than antipiracy. He was tied into a criminal network and just finished checking a hidden website that listed the ships under target in the strait. The pirates knew the *Green Dog* was associated with the Chinese Triad; therefore, the *Green Dog* was off-limits. No need to pick a fight with another criminal gang. But the Captain took the appropriate countermeasures. *Loyalties change. There is no law to enforce* on *the high seas, and with an absence of law and order, there is anarchy* at sea. *In his book, there are no enforceable laws in international waters, and pirates better beware of his crew. He reflected on the time his crew killed six pirates with Mossberg pump-action shotguns. Yes, the Green Dog had a reputation,* he thought. He listened to a twangy Malaysian tune on the VHF Radio. The pirates kept a microphone keyed open next to an AM radio playing the music. A ship calling a distress would be blocked unless it had a more powerful signal than the pirates, which they did not. *After three "drunken nights" in Kuala Lumpur, the crew can finally get some rest when we get out of the straits.* . . . Unbeknownst to the Captain, the *Jinryu* waited, in the middle of the South China Sea, for the ship to pass Singapore and turn north toward Vladivostok.

Chen and Don swam a slow stroke smoothly through the warm water. The ship, moving at eighteen knots, would come to them. Visibility was zero in the inky darkness, but they could make out the regulation navigation lights and outline of the massive ship before them. From a mesh sack waist pack, the two commandos removed electromagnetic suction cups. The noise from the ship grew louder, and Chen actually thought they would be hit as eighteen knots seemed very fast when the ship was upon them. Chen's respirations increased as he back swam away, least the ship hit him. It was like looking up at a superstructure, except that the superstructure was moving at a fast clip, while they were moving toward it and trying not to be sucked in, caught in the wake, or slammed against the side. Still, the two were strong swimmers, and had experience approaching large vessels at sea. Then the two swam back into the moving ship, attaching the suction cups to the hull. Instantly, they felt the sense of safety as the device locked to the hull. They both held the suction cups with a handle on the end. Pushing a button with his thumb, the cup released and Chen placed it higher on the hull. He released the other cup when the higher cup was attached. The hardest part was the initial attachment and climb out of the ship's wake. Once out of the water, they used one hand to remove their flippers. They no longer needed them. Now it became a feat of upper body strength as they climbed straight up the hull. One minute later they peered cautiously over the dark deck of the ship. They already knew the deck was clear of crew because the *Jinryu* launched a small surveillance RPA (remote piloted aircraft) that maintained a tight circular flight pattern around the *Green Dog*. An RPA Sensor Operator on the *Jinryu* controlled the RPA, watched live video feed on a nanocrystal monitor, and had communication with the two-man team through a small earpiece they wore. The earpiece acted as a personal sound amplification device that allowed the *Jinryu* to monitor audio at all times. The deck lights remained off and the entire crew was asleep, except the pilot in the bridge and one man in the engine room. The ship was out of pirate country and this was their first night of good rest. At Tsukuba Space Center in Japan, Sumiko Albright, Don's mother, like a lioness protecting her cub, watched her only son board the vessel.

They dropped the suction cups overboard and removed a Beretta 21 from their shoulder holster that was over a ⅛ inch wetsuit and twisted silencers to the weapons, hoping they would not use the pistols. The dirty white color wetsuits matched the paint scheme of most cargo ships and oil tankers. The upper portion of the wetsuit made from a combination of a special neoprene mixed with Kevlar and could stop a bullet from a small caliber handgun. Don looked at Chen and he could feel the fear, the fear they both felt. But they turned the fear into a buzz, a buzz, like a high, that kept them in the profession they were in and always coming back for more. Chen was familiar with the *Green Dog* from a 1999 U.S. Customs boarding in Bodega Bay, and he quickly moved among the stacked cargo containers until he found the large opening to the cargo compartment. The opening was large enough for a crane to raise and lower large cargo items. Don removed fifty feet of black purlon rope from his small backpack, tied a figure-eight knot in one end, and handed the knot to Chen. Chen snapped the knot into a carabiner he had attached to a ring on a cargo container. Don made a half-hitch knot, snapped it in a carabiner on his dive belt, and repelled deep into the depths of the cargo hold. Chen followed seven seconds later.

"In cargo hold," Don whispered in Japanese into a watch-like devise on his wrist. "Looks clear." He wore a night-vision contact lens in his left eye. In the event of sudden bright light, the left eye would be blinded until he removed the lens.

"Good job. Deck is clear," Commander Kano, onboard the *Jinryu*, replied back. He looked at his watch. *Fifty seconds and they were in the cargo compartment. Not even a minute on the deck. Damn they are good.*

Chen knew exactly where he wanted to go and what he was going to do. It was eerie and dark in the hold, an immense man-made cavern filled with various types of cargo. Halfway through the football size cargo hold the two relaxed a little. The two appeared like ghost, moving fast and in file without speaking. Chen knew, from the 1999 customs after-action report, a false wall existed in the aft portion of the cargo compartment. U.S. Customs left the hide-out in place hoping to score a big catch in the future. Ironically, the *Green Dog* stayed out of U.S. ports after the 1999 incident. He guessed at once at the suspected false wall location, running one hand lightly over a raised lip next to the wall he found a small latch. As vibrations rattled within the hold, he threw the wall open with the latch.

The dim red light from Don's penlight barely revealed four persons huddled in the corner. The sight sent a wave of acid horror into Don's gut. The sudden unexpected sight of humans when you expect to find inanimate objects terrified the two. The four were just girls, barely in their teens. They faced each other. No one had ever pointed a loaded pistol at them, and they stared at the commandos. Huddled in the corner, one girl squirmed and whimpered in the older girls lap.

"*Salamat Datang*! *Salamat Datang*!" Don said in a loud whisper. He was not sure what the words meant in Malaysian. He remembered the greeting spoken by flight attendants when he boarded a Malaysian Air flight. Don's words seemed to calm the situation.

"Stowaways," Chen said. "Stowaways."

The girls couldn't run--they couldn't hide. They felt the panic of a trapped animal. With sudden desperation, the older girl stood and opened her hand, revealing a necklace with a gold cross. Her hands were shaking. She was weak with fear. Her squeaky voice cut like a razor. "Gold! You GOLD!" She said in agitated jerks of English.

There was tense silence. As for the young Malaysian women, they were under the impression they were going to be waitresses in respectable Vladivostok restaurants. They had worked in a shoe factory before they'd accepted the misleading job offers from a member of the Chinese Triad. And now, more than ever, the girls admitted to each other that they'd had moments of doubt. They simply encountered many bad men aboard the ship.

"Let's go," Chen said, backing out of the concealed area and closing the false wall. He looked across the dark cargo hold and saw nothing but the outline of stacked pallets of various dry goods. "Sorry, I thought we would find 'PBFs' in the false wall," Chen said, and gave an embarrassed little laugh. "You lead, I'll follow."

Don backtracked toward their entry point. Using his night-vision contact lens, Don weaved at remarkable speed through the pallets with goods piled perilously high. Chen, unable to see clearly stayed close to Don. Suddenly, Don stopped--he acted purely on instinct, using his one eye like a powerful magnifying glass.

Chen could feel Don's aura cut through the darkness; it was if he were somehow exploding. And when Don's voice came, it reverberated in Chen's head like thunder.

"Shoygu! Shoygu!"

Chen's instincts, which never failed him, told him the "PBFs" were located in the wooded crates with SHOYGU stenciled on the side. Within two minutes, they discovered an exorbitant amount of "PBFs" mixed in with a sword shipment. Chen removed several notes from various bundles and secured then in sealed plastic pouches. He then removed a can of spray from Don's pack and began spraying the bills with a colorless, odorless mist, a detection substance that CIRO developed. Sumiko had the can airdropped from a Japanese business Lear Jet to the *Jenryu*. Chen never used the spray before but trusted Sumiko. This was not what Chen wanted to do—he wanted to destroy the "PBF's" to prevent their circulation. But someone other than himself called "the shots." The "shot-caller," whoever it was, was unknown to him.

Chen put the spray can in his pack, zipped it closed, and turned to Don. Don secured webbing back over the crates. All they wanted right now was to get the hell off the *Green Dog*. When they were done, the two moved away fast.

It was dim, not dark, by the rope used in the rappel. Don began the climb-up the rope first. A thin light, from a flashlight with bad batteries, filtered across the opening above Don. "Trouble! Someone is walking on the deck," Kanto's voice came in low in Don's earpiece. Chen heard it too. Don froze. He wrapped his leg around the rope to preserve upper body strength. His grip was strong and sure, but climbing a ½" purlon rope is not easy.

Don's dark brown eye, aided by the contact lens, spotted a group of uniform pallets located on the opposite side where they previously had been. The pallets were all the same size and covered with black plastic. Three years ago, Don met Chen and Sam Young at Yokota Air Base. The two were on a special mission, code-named "*Black Opal*," escorting U.S. currency to Japan. The aircraft was loaded with pallets of "black plastic." It was no secret where currency was printed, but how money got from point A to point B was a highly classified secret of the Federal Reserve. Don slid down the rope.

"I saw something. I want to check it out," Don whispered to Chen. He then whispered a quick message into his wrist device.

"Okay," Chen said. His voice was calm, but Don saw the look on Chen's face that signaled "it better be quick." Then Don moved with the delicacy of a man using slick stepping stones to cross a swift stream.

The pallets gleamed a greasy green-black through Don's contact lens. Chen looked alarmed at the sight of the "Black Plastic" cargo. He counted eighteen airlift pallets, all approximately seventy inches in height with a web top-net over the cargo to secure it. Chen peeled back the plastic through the web netting to reveal neatly stacked "PBFs." Chen visualized the carts of money stacked in the football sized vault, the second largest vault in the world, in the basement of the Federal Reserve in Los Angles. He attempted to make a comparison.

"There must be about ½ of what is in the vault in LA in these pallets!" He gasped. The words ran perfectly out of his mouth like soldiers in a column. "Get word to your mother that the *Green Dog* is 5 times bigger than '*Black Opal,*' repeat 5 times bigger." Chen's face was still amazed, and he found it hard to comprehend.

Don nodded, spoke into his wrist device and relayed the message.

Chen looked at his watch and saw that thirty-four minutes had passed since they boarded the ship.

Five minutes later, the two jumped off the *Green Dog* in the "man overboard" position taught to all sailors in basic training. Not four minutes later, the *Jenryu* surfaced to recover the two commandos. They were not aware that their discovery set in motion events that would lead to the overthrow of a dictatorship. But Commander Kano's intuition told him there was more to this mission. *Jenryu* just received orders sending the vessel into very serious waters above the 38th Parallel in the Yellow Sea.

Director Mike Perry got the word before the Deputy Director of the Korean Central Intelligence Agency (KCIA) did. Sumiko Albright, Deputy Director, CIRO, called him directly to brief him on Chen's mission, and she assured him he was safe, but would be out of contact for a few days. She relayed this information along with digital files on a dead FSB agent, a dead Chinese Triad gang member, and the possible location of the missing Malaysian Boeing 777-200. The missing triple seven did not come as a shock to Mike Perry because of information gathered from a well-placed agent in Russia--the media believed the jet to have crashed in the Indian Ocean. *Now, he began to understand what "the Pamphlet" by Putin critic, Boris Nemtsov, may contain.* He would have to let this work out. He did not want to jeopardize his agent. In addition, Sumiko mentioned something about a "PBF" but was not sure what it meant. She stressed the urgency of the situation and the possible Russian/North Korean plans for another airliner incident. It turned out that the three agency heads knew each other well. Sumiko had already developed a crisis plan and was confident the KCIA would developed their own plan. But it was the news of the magnitude of counterfeits on the *Green Dog* that disturbed the Director. After talking with Sumiko, the Director rubbed his eyes and glanced around the silent room that was essentially a fortress. Although the room was windowless and soundproof, it was capable of being bugged. Mike had learned from TJ that the Russians had managed to place a bug in his office. Years ago, the Russians and Americans played the cold-war game. *Well, the "game" was on again and more deadly with higher stakes*, Perry contemplated as he switched his thoughts to the *Green Dog*.

Mike Perry wanted to stop the *Green Dog*. Lately, the timidity and reluctance of President Obama infuriated him. He suspected the President would not take action, particularly since it involved Putin. Obama would urge "strategic patience," and the ship would sail into Vladivostok. He did not like questioning the loyalty of the President of the United States, the President that appointed him. Perry dialed a direct line to Sumiko Albright. She answered on the first ring. "We cannot let the *Green Dog* port in Vladivostok." Perry said and waited.

"Fine, the Seventh Fleet can escort it to any port in Japan. You have our support."

"I cannot predict what the President will do, but I think he will do nothing," Mike Perry continued. "Can you work with the Koreans and port the ship in Pusan?"

"Okay, I will look into it. What is your take on the Malaysian airliner hijacking?" Sumiko understood the position Mike was in. She had to 'cover' for the Americans on matters relating with the Mossad. *What is wrong with Obama*, she thought.

"All I will say is I am beginning to piece together the puzzle. Sumiko, I suspect a falling out 'of sort' with the President over this issue. I will take a vacation. You must trust me. I will be working a plan that will change the course of history for Asia. That is all I will say for now. Can you port the *Green Dog* in Pusan and maintain secrecy of the 'supernotes' from the media?" Mike Perry asked as his mind began to focus on his next task, talking to the President, a man that wanted to know everything about political enemies, yet all his personal records were sealed by court order before running for President.

"I will do my best," she paused. "Mike, how is Sam Young? I have not heard from him," she asked. Somehow Sumiko suspected Sam would play a role in "Mike's Plan," whatever it was.

There was a long delay before Mike spoke, "He is fine. Thank you, Sumiko." Mike hung up the phone, thinking that some sort of message passed between the two.

After September 11th, Sumiko spearheaded various discussions between Japan's Military Space Forces and the Japanese Defense Forces on sea denial strategy, that is, the ability to deny a ship's access to various ports. With the intention of curbing North Korea's nuclear ambitions, a strategy was put in place by both the government and the military that was structured toward preventing ships from porting in North Korea. The strategy was in-place but had never been implemented. Sea denial was achieved through ECM (electronic countermeasures) aircraft, *Atago* class destroyers, and Japan's two advanced imagery satellites and four electro-optical (EO) satellites. In short, a vessel's navigation, along with communications, were hacked into and given erroneous data.

Unbeknown to the *Green Dog* Captain and crew, the ship navigated a circular area east of Pusan for eighteen hours before turning directly toward Pusan. By the time the Captain realized he should have done the thinking instead of the ship's computers, the *Green Dog* lost all power—the ship was towed, under escort by the ROK (Republic of Korea) Navy, to the Port of Pusan.

On July 24, 2014, *The Korean Times* reported the *Green Dog* was under a 10-day quarantine pending the unexplained death at sea of the entire crew.

Chapter 15

Moscow

July 15, 2014

Putin arrived in the Kremlin at 0845 for the 0900 meeting. He stopped at the brick structure to talk with the saluting soldiers of the 4th Guards Kantemirov tank Division, the same elite unit that had been positioned along the Ukrainian border since March 12th, over four months. The subject of his mother baking stuffed buns (pirozhki) with cabbage, meat, and rice came up with the soldiers. Putin told his aide to look into getting fresh pirozhki to the troops on the border. The gesture was noticed by people outside the Kremlin. Taking the stone steps instead of the elevator, Putin made his way to the second floor. Like a leopard, he bounded up the steps, followed by his aide, Colonel Vasily Borov, who tried to stay up with him.

Within Russia, and the world, everyone knew who ran Russia, the same man who ran the country even when his term limits expired. It was as if his ruling was foreordained as the falling of snow on the Kremlin. As long as he was alive and in good health, he would rule Russia. This was understood and no one objected.

Putin took his seat at the front of the long table reserved for ministers and Politburo members. The July 15th meeting consisted of only two men: the Director of the FSB and the Head of the Ministry of Defense. Both men were billionaires and considered the two most powerful men in Russia, besides Putin. The general of the FSB made his millions as director of the largest shipping company in Russia. Shipping, an area of personal interest to Putin, is the perfect business for moving products around the world, including counterfeit money, drugs, and gold. One of the deputies of the Central Bank accused the Director of money-laundering. Shortly thereafter, the bank official was murdered by a gunshot wound to the head. The Defense Minister collected cold weapons: swords, daggers, broadswords; Chinese, Japanese, and Samurai swords. The collection was valued at over forty million dollars. He was a man that brought credence to the saying, *Live by the Sword, die by the Sword.*

"Vladimir, look what I have for you," the defense minister beamed as he set a knife with a crescent curved blade on the table. "This is a 16th Century Karambit knife from Indonesian. It is my gift to you."

"Thank you, Sergei, Thank you. Can I use it to skin trout on our next fishing trip?" Putin glanced down at the knife, showing interest because Sergei was one of his closest protégés. Putin picked up the knife, inspecting it. Then he remembered Chul moo telling him how he killed the Malaysian Airline pilot with a Karambit knife. Sweat broke out on his forehead.

"Vladimir, you can use it for whatever you wish. Why you can cut cabbage if you so desire."

Putin knew he would need all of his intellect to steer the two men over to his view. "The reforms you made increasing the officer corps is working out well."

"An increase in the officer corps requires an increase in soldiers to command. The military modernization will soon put us above Soviet era levels," Sergei promised.

Putin nodded. "We will be needing a large army. Will the office corps be ready in time for 'Fortress Crimea,' Sergei? He continued checking the knife out as he spoke.

"I think so. Our naval upgrades are ahead of schedule, particularly the Black Sea Fleet," Sergei said with a gentle voice and benign smile. "I think 'Fortress Crimea' will strangulate the Ukrainians in a manner similar to Lincoln's Anaconda Policy that strangled the South during the American Civil war." Sergei's calmness, a devout Buddhist, all designed to mesmerize the prey in front of him.

Putin's robust voice asked, "Sergei, do you know the saying about Russia and the Ukraine?"

There was a bitter laugh. "Of course, Russia is merely a country without Ukraine, but with Ukraine, Russia is an empire!"

"Yes! Sergei, you will be rewarded for 'Fortress Crimea.' Medvedev is tired and has expressed a desire to move on. Perhaps in the future you could become Prime Minister. That way when my term is up we can flip-flop. You know, keep the continuity of the empire going." Putin nodded his head, his cold face cloudy with unspoken worries. "You are confident in 'Fortress Crimea' I take it," asked Putin. "And how are the upgrades to our Spetsnaz units coming?"

"Absolutely! Lands battles in Ukraine are nothing compared to what will happen when we shut off Ukraine from the sea. It is a move from A.T Mahan's *The Influence of SEA POWER upon History*. Our land connection to Crimea will make Ukraine a land bird, unable to fly far from shore." Sergei's slanted eyes and dark complexion remained focused on Putin. "We will do well with our special ops units integrated with the use of drones for surveillance and targeting, not to mention the use of electronic warfare, an area of operations we will implement on a major scale for the first time."

"And Crimea will become our launch pad for operations in the south, Eastern Europe," Alexander stated flatly. "I am ramping up FSB security centres 16 & 18, operating out of Skolkovo, for information warfare and terrorist activities, like city bombings, if need be."

"Yes, asymmetric warfare in the Baltics will break NATO," Putin hunched forward toward the two men. "Which brings me to another point—Afghanistan."

"Afghanistan?" questioned the FSB Director, Putin's old KGB partner, Alexander, suddenly becoming alert.

"We lost in Afghanistan for the same reason the Americans lost in Vietnam— public support. After the meeting with the Politburo and ministers, it is agreed that we will step up activity in Ukraine. Rostov is ready. We will soon fire artillery across the border, engage in air-to-air combat, move heavy-caliber artillery, and move powerful multiple rocket launchers into towns throughout eastern and southern Ukraine," Putin said calmly.

"You have the confidence of us all and public support is at an all-time high," the director purred in his smooth, salesman's voice.

"Yes, for now. The bodies of our boys in ski masks are coming back to Russia. As the war goes on, as it will, the public support will wane. I am not concerned about world opinion. I am only concerned with mother Russia. We must keep our eye on the goal.

The goal of reversing current policy and returning to Soviet levels of strategic territory, departing from the notions of strategic stability of the status-quo." Putin looked grave.

The defense minister pondered. "There must be a huge change in the perception of a friendly environment and the presence of external threat, then a change of perceptions can cause a change in posture planning as well."

"Exactly!" Putin declared, "The state of affairs now is such that we cannot even produce our own ships. We are buying from the French. Our primary goal is to concentrate all weapons and the industrial base in Russia. We are a great nation with an abundance of natural resources and talented people. We do not need Europe. Actually Europe needs us more than we need them. Tomorrow the Americans will hit us with sanctions. Europe will follow suit to appease the Americans. The 28 European Union members cannot agree on anything. They will apply sanctions also but to a smaller extend. They know how cold the winters get in Germany."

"The sanctions are nothing. Merely lip service to appease the media. We have already moved assets out of London, Brussels, and New York. I, myself, will be targeted with an asset freeze. I moved ninety-percent of funds before we went into Crimea," Alexander said.

"It is absolute lunacy for the Europeans to impose sanctions, because we will counter with hampering cooperation with terrorism and organized crime. Why I predict airliners will get hijacked and fall out of the sky. The French and Germans are making a huge mistake by going along with the Americans," Putin said, while shooting an irritated glance at the men, then smiled and inspected his knife blade at the table again. "At a time of the Arab uprisings and us in charge of rogue states, Europe is shooting itself in the foot," Putin pointed out. "However, the Russian economy faces a dire situation in the near future should oil fall to $75 a barrel, as predicted. The sanctions on specific Russian sectors will hurt. Global political instability does help keep the price of oil inflated. We need a "game changer," and I know what it is."

"Without our help on terrorism, it is certain Europe will get hit with a 9/11 magnitude attack. This will keep the price of oil above what it is now. What is it now? I believe $110 per barrel," Alexander mused.

Sergei caught a faint glint in Putin's eye. "What is it Vladimir?"

There was a time for bluntness. "I propose we shoot-down an airliner over Ukraine to restore us to a Soviet-centric/Russian-centric way of thinking." Putin fixed his unblinking hard stare on the two men.

The director inclined his head in acknowledgement. "An undertaking of this nature will require absolute secrecy. The opposition, this Boris Nemtsov, is trouble for us. If the opposition movement 'caught wind' of this."

"Secrecy is what has made us great. Secrecy keeps Russia all but opaque to the West," the collector of cold weapons said.

"That is why I came to you two. In this situation the *zapiska*, or memorandum system of decision-making will not work. The process is slow and interagency fighting would go on and on." A flat statement by Putin.

Sergei stiffened. "Interesting. The shoot-down could easily be perceived as a mistake by the separatist. Vladimir, you are a master tactician with an eye on the 'grand prize' for *Rodina*!"

"Sergei, you would know the details and how to carry this out better than anyone," Putin said pleasantly. "And has for Nemtsov. We will squish him like a fly should he persist with supporting Ukraine. Alexander, I believe you can handle Nemtsov."

"We can easily round up a handful of 'undesirable' Chechens from the North Caucasus and tie them to murder. I maintain a list, Vladimir. It is no problem. It will be done," Alexander looked over to Sergei when he saw concern on his face.

Sergei nodded his head, indicating his approval for removing Nemtsov. "Yes, and the movement will die. But more importantly is oil. Some economist believe oil will drop below fifty dollars per barrel. Can we weather such a drop in oil?"

"We can and I have a contingency for just that scenario. Let me say, I have made an arrangement for an unlimited amount of U.S. currency that will be laundered around the world. That is all I will say on that for now," Putin cautioned. "We will give the appearance to the world that low oil prices, economic sanctions, and condemnation from the downed airliner is crippling us. After our quasi-invasion of eastern Ukraine, we launch the full-scale invasion of Ukraine. This will trigger a huge geopolitical crisis with NATO—it will shock the price of oil back up. And I have another plan to raise the price of oil. Alexander, I take it you still maintain your contacts in the shipping industry."

Alexander nodded. "Of course. Our shipping business is through, should I say, associates. It allows us to maintain anonymity under ships flying flags of convenience, it makes perfect sense--this way details remain murky. This transparency has been instrumental in exporting nuclear technology to Iran and North Korea, not to mention arms, drugs, or whatever." But as he talked he noticed Putin's aura had an unhealthy appearance that bordered on frightening. For the first time, Alexander thought perhaps Putin had some mental condition. There was something in his eyes that was not right. Alexander thought it was a good time to "make Putin happy" so he would stay in his good graces. "It is an ocean world, it is lawless and wild. On another note, I have some good news on 'snowbird,' Vladimir."

"Oh, you mean the NSA (National Security Agency) employee we granted asylum to last year," Putin asked.

"The one and only. The revelations we gathered from him has been instrumental in setting up a huge computer hacking ring. This ring will operate from Eastern Europe and hack into banks across Europe and the United States," Alexander gave Putin an intense, pleading look.

"Can the hacking be traced to us?" Putin smiled and took a deep breath.

"The ingenious part of the operation is the majority of the hacking will be against banks in Russia. We will steal from ourselves and no it cannot be traced to us. By the time the banks catch on it will be too late. We would have already stolen millions, maybe into the billions. We use a special router that reroutes signals across 6,000 servers to hide page request's origin, making clicks on illicit material nearly impossible for the best law enforcement to trace. I will await your order before launchings the operation."

"You done good Alexander with this 'Snowbird.' We will hold on this operation until the Americans put the squeeze on us over Ukraine. In the meantime, I want you to increase trade with North Korea. Let's say a 30% increase in ships into North Korean ports over a period of the next year. We are going to get out of supplying arms to proxies, mainly Syria." Putin held his stare another moment, as if boring into the two men to see what they were made of.

"Understood. But the weapons/ammunition make their way to the Islamic Extremists in Iraq. This is a huge headache for the Americans," Alexander commented. "At any rate, our network of invitation-only chat rooms and forums, hidden behind alphanumeric addresses, provides access to the most elite circle of criminals."

Putin clearly saw Alexander's excitement on his cyberterrorism activities and committed himself to sit down with Alexander in private and learn more. "The Americans will keep their headache because our Communist brothers in North Korea will supply Syria. Our supplying the weapons is a 'thorn in the side' to the Saudis. Through secret talks with the Saudi Prince, who will soon become the King, he has agreed to boost the price of oil if we stop supplying Syria. Also, eventually, the Americans will want to supply lethal weapons to Ukraine. American anti-tank Javelin missiles would dramatically improve the situation on the ground for the Ukrainians. We maintain a stronger position in the 'poker game' if we are out of supplying to proxies. And I have a plan for increasing currency to a few select banks. It may be able to tie in with the bank hacking. We will look at it." Putin's tone was corpselike, returning to the airliner: "Are you in in? Are you with me on the airliner?"

For a time, the three sat silently, Putin's steady gaze fixed on the two, obviously assembling their thoughts. When the words came, once more what they did *not* say carried the real meaning: "We could never admit to committing this act. The downing of an airliner."

Putin heard the unsaid. "Europe and the United States will implicate us but not hold us directly responsible. The condemnation of the world against us will galvanize Russians and instill nationalism—restoring a Russian-centric perception."

"When do you want to do this?" Sergei asked.

"Two days from now, July 17, MH17 Flight."

Both men nodded.

Putin smiled. "Thank you, gentlemen. That, I think, concludes our meeting."

They both stood, nodding their head again, and walked out of the office into the large hallway. The deal was sealed, and they left the office knowing an airliner would be shot down and Nemtsov would be killed, and it was the right thing, and also the best thing for everyone in Russia.

Putin watched them go. For some reason, he remembered the Opening Ceremony at Sochi when the Ukrainian athletes received a huge applause. *Yes, Sergei was right. Perceptions must change. Malaysian Airlines, like Sochi, would be a chance for self-promotion--more global attention.*

Chapter 16

Eastern Ukraine

July 17, 2014

Spetsnaz, the Russian highly-trained saboteurs, spies, and special operations forces that secured Crimea—and the borders—of Ukraine escorted Lieutenant Colonel Bezler into eastern Ukraine. Lt. Col. Bezler, a spit-and-polish senior officer normally worn a spotless uniform along with a clean-shaven face, with the Russian Air Defense Forces, never operated like this before during his eighteen year career. He felt like a hoodlum among a group of misfits. But the four men escorting him were not misfits, and this he ascertained by the respect they showed toward him, a senior officer in the Russian Air Defense Forces.

Just six months earlier Bezler, known as "the devil," finished at the top of his class at Marshal Leonid Govorov Air Defense and Radio Engineering Academy, the graduate school for senior commissioned officers in the Air Defense Force. He studied innovations in radar, aerospace defense, and surface-to-air missile systems and received a Masters of Electrical Systems Engineering degree.

"Why do they call you the devil? You seem like a book smart computer guy to me," the driver of the GAZ-2975 all-terrain vehicle asked.

"Now how did you find that out?"

"Sir, we like to know a little information about our mission. We asked around," Anton answered.

"Fair enough," Bezler replied. "The Minister of Defense gave me that name because I won the big snowmobile race in Siberia three years in a row. He thinks I cheat by going off the course, so he nicknamed me 'the devil' and it stuck."

"Did you?"

"What?"

"Did you cheat?" *If this guy knows the Minister of Defense this is a higher profile mission than he believed*, thought Anton.

"Well let's just say I am good with Geometry, speed, distance, and finding short cuts!" Bezler chuckled. "Hey, what kind of engine is in this thing?"

"I forget the horsepower. It's an American engine, a company called Cummins. I like the wolf vehicle better. The Israelis make the wolf," Anton replied with his own smile. He checked his watch again. "We will be there soon, sir."

"The Israelis? I didn't know we are buying vehicles from the Israelis," Bezler said, looking at all the damaged vacant buildings.

"We're not buying them. We stole four wolves from the Georgians. Georgia buys from the Israelis."

"I didn't know we are in Georgia," Bezler replied, checking his watch and noting the cloud cover.

"We are everywhere."

Finally the truck grumbled to a stop in a field, next to a SA-11, surface-to-air missile site. The three other Spetsnaz troops appeared at the rear of the vehicle. Not far from the SAM site, Bezler saw two trucks, each surrounded by a group of men, smoking and milling about, bolt-action rifles dangling from their shoulders. The men's weapons told Bezler they were separatist.

"Okay, where is my crew?" Bezler asked.

Four of the young men by the trucks immediately came over. They began bragging about how well they knew the missile system, claiming to have shot down two planes.

Bezler looked at his watch, 1540 hours. The TOT (time on target) was around 1600 hours. He hated to turn-on, or light-up, the system too early for fear of getting shot. But he had to trust his intelligence. "Everyone take your position. I only need three men. I will occupy the command vehicle," he ordered. The men moved to the target acquisition radar (TAR) vehicle, the transporter erector launcher, and radar (TELAR and TEL) vehicles.

Bezler crab-walked into the tight fitting command vehicle. He powered it up, got on headset, and began what he called his pre-flight. He immediately was pleased to see this was a Buk-M1, which was a 1998 upgrade of the command vehicle. *This was going to be a walk-in-the-park,* he thought, *already knowing the altitude and timing made his job easy. "Battle management," the overall general knowledge of the tactical environment, that is, where the enemy is supposed to be is the hard part. "Oh...there it was on radar,"* he said to himself. *It was about right with proper geometry between the radar and target.* Under most circumstances, the self-propelled mount detects the target, determined its IFF (Identify Friend or Foe) status, automatically tracked the target and identified its type, computes the flight mission and launch assignment, and launches the missile. This launch was different in that it was not an automatic launch, but a manual launch. The IFF interrogator interpreted the target as a friendly. There was no jamming to distort the data generated. Bezler quickly deciphered the jet engine modulation, it was a high bypass ratio engine with larger slower fans. *It was an airliner! No, it could not be an airliner, it must be an American C-5 or C-17. They often* used the same IFF squawk codes as airliners. With Russia stepping up operations, the Americans would get more involved. The "devil" pushed the launch button. Within a minute the system verified the kill. Bezler powered the system down and exited the command vehicle.

The Spetsnaz troops gave a bottle of Nemiroff Vodka to the separatist soldiers. Bezler saw the bottle was already half-empty as they passed it back and forth.

"Sir, our orders are to return you to Russia. We need to get going. This area is going to get hot."

The GAZ all-terrain truck left eastern Ukraine around 1620 hours. Bezler slept while driving into Russia and awoke in time to watch the setting sun. He thought of the Siberia snowmobile races, and vowed to race and win again. *I can't wait to see my good friend Boris Nemtsov. He has an interest in Ukraine and will know details about the aircraft I just shot out of the sky.*

Chapter 17

Jekyll Island

August 1, 2014

On vacation, wearing a disguise that included a full-length beard, Mike Perry departed Washington D.C. under the cover of darkness. He stealthily drove south into Georgia and onto an island deserted by all but a few employees of the Federal Reserve. He was stopped by four construction workers that appeared also to be part of a security detail, on the paved causeway that provided the only access to the island. Perry flashed his CIA badge, not saying much, but implying he was Mr. Secret Squirrel himself, all the while looking at the heavy machinery.

"Mr. Perry, you are the last one. We have been waiting for you. We are to make sure you get through from here to the hotel. This causeway will be closed for repairs.

You can proceed to the Jekyll Island Club Hotel," the foreman said, smiling weakly, while nodding his head toward two men sitting on backhoe loaders. The men swung into motion by starting the machines.

The car moved forward onto the isolated island. In his rearview mirror, Perry saw a bulldozer and signs block the road, and the two backhoes began tearing the road apart. It was ironic that the island itself, the same place the Federal Reserve System was created, was chosen as the place to resolve the "financial crisis" tied to North Korea and Russia. He looked forward to getting some rest before the meetings started. His agenda included a TOP SECRET Conference to discuss the problem of the "PBF" that threatened American Finance and arrive at a solution before leaving Jekyll Island. He, more than any man, held the ultimate counter-punch to Kim Jong un.

It was ten in the morning, the hour noted by the low, echoing chimes of the grandfather clock, surrounded by statues, mixed with Queen Anne furniture from the early 20th Century in the large suite. The heads of six men seated around an ornate mahogany circular table in the Presidential Suite turned in unison to listen to Alan Blackspan.

"Mr. Perry, I hope you find the accommodations meet your satisfaction," Alan Blackspan remarked, the ex-chairman of the Federal Reserve for nineteen years, "does the secure communications room fulfill your requirements?"

"Yes, it is fine. I have already used it. Thank you," Perry answered, smiling, as he looked at the décor and opulence of the Presidential Suite in the Jekyll Island Club Hotel. *He had come a long ways from the days as an Army officer on the DMZ.*

"The Federal Reserve," explained Alan Blackspan, "is the bedrock of world finance. It's an American Institution created to foster the free flow of capital on markets around the world. It is under attack from North Korea and Russia by the production of the so called 'PBFs,' or Perfect Ben Franklin."

"I'm sorry, I thought the new Federal Reserve Notes countered the North Korean 'supernotes.'. . . How long have the 'PBFs' been in circulation?" asked William Johns, the head of the San Francisco District, the economic powerhouse for Asian Commerce. The San Francisco District evolved to become the 21st Century central banking system, thus making Johns a powerful candidate for position of Chairman of the Federal Reserve in the future.

"Please, Director Perry, enlighten us," said Allan Blackspan, frowning, disturbed. "Brief us on what you know or don't know."

"I'm afraid it is far worse than we imagined," he said quietly, breathing deeply to find his own control. "We estimate the Kim regime came out with the PBFs six to eight months after we first printed our new note. Unbeknownst to the Russians, a Japanese commando team boarded a North Korean cargo vessel at sea that was destined for Vladivostok and discovered a large shipment of PBFs mixed in with a large order of 'cold weapons' addressed to the Russian Defense Minister. The Russians--" Perry stopped abruptly, and his eyes narrowed. He took in all the faces at the table. "The Russians ordered the shoot-down of MH17!" Without an instant of pause and with consideration, Perry set fire to the bridge he had just crossed.

A murmur of both disbelief and shock traveled around the table.

"Do we have enough hard evidence to implicate the Russians?" William Johns asked. His voice was steady. "The *Green Dog* in Pusan. Can you fill us in on the ship's *contents*?"

"The information is from Dave Chen out of your district, Mr. Johns. And there is the backing of CIRO, Japanese Intelligence. The proof is in the intelligence report before your eyes. Chen estimates the *Green Dog* contains between 13-15 Billion U.S., in 'PBFs'. The ship is under quarantine," said Perry without a flicker. Then he glanced at his notes, anticipating the questions.

"Who else is aware of the 'PBFs?" Johns asked. He stared into Perry's eyes, searching for deception, but could find none, just worry, which concerned him. "Is it true the entire crew died at sea, as reported by the press?"

"Deputy Director Albright with CIRO, and Deputy Director Yi with the KCIA. I assume a small number of their staff working the crisis. And of course Putin and Kim

Jong un. The KCIA Intel on North Korea is the best. I suspect they have HUMINT (Human Intelligence) resources in-country. We have an agent in-place in Russia and await word from him." Perry said smoothly, giving his voice credibility. "Our Secret Service is not even aware of the PBFs. I can assure you Albright and Yi will keep quiet while they await word from us."

"Director, I commend you on your efforts working with Korea and Japan on regional security matters. This was clearly an incredible intelligence operation conducted by the Koreans and Japanese. You have also done a remarkable job working with Canadian and Israeli intelligence," Johns finished softly, ignoring Perry not answering his question about the crew. Johns respected his reluctance. As magicians clings to their mystique, so the top spook is secretive about the operation.

Then a memory resurfaced in Perry's mind, a memory of the IRA safe house on the shore of Lake Ontario—it had been a connection that led to a failed assassination attempt on Osama bin Laden. Remembering that was like opening the door of the 9/11 closet—only what came out was the avalanche of intelligence blunders.

"Director Perry, can you go over President Obama's reaction to this crisis," Blackspan inquired, while he stared at Perry, then turned his colorless gaze to the middle of the Mahogany table, as if studying the grains in the wood.

Politics was the last thing Perry wanted to get invoked with in the Obama Administration. But in the end analysis, it was Politics that placed him in his job, and he assumed it would be politics that removed him.

Blackspan waited for Perry's crucial answer. "The President did not view the matter as a great concern. He did not see the threat to our financial institution. The President did not want to antagonize Putin. He instructed me to maintain patience and not involve the Koreas or Japanese. He failed to grasp that it was the Japanese that provided the initial intelligence on the *Green Dog*," Perry insisted. "I was instructed to take some time off, take a vacation. I suspect I will be replaced, asked to retire, or resign."

"I see," said Blackspan, puzzled by the President's lack of concern. He had sheets of Federal Reserve figures before him and was studying them while he spoke.

"Replaced?" Johns echoed, as if replacement was out of the question. "You are one of the prime architects on the killing of Bin laden. The way I read the commission report, 9/11 would not have happened if we followed your assessment."

"Gentlemen, therein lies the problem, the Obama Administration and leaks? There is bound to be leaks soon. The U.S. Dollar is the bedrock of financial security for the entire free world. We all know it is merely a fiat currency. It is mere paper backed up by nothing but the faith and security of the United States. As you know, I have been an advocate for the gold standard, but I lost that fight years ago. Our entire financial system is under direct attack and will crumble unless we do something. Thus, the importance of this meeting." Blackspan frowned.

Eric Adelman, the retired CEO of GS Bank, nicknamed Government Sachs, now President of the New York Branch, nodded unhappily. "How good is the information, Director? One hundred percent? Eighty?"

A momentary silence. "Because of your actions, that is, forming a North Korean Division in the mid-eighties to follow 'supernotes,' I say the information is One hundred percent accurate. Sam Young and Dave Chen have been instrumental in the 'supernote' fight. And with my plan the two will play a vital role in solving this crisis," Perry said. But he barely heard what he was saying. The excitement was thudding away in his chest and at his temples like a second heartbeat.

"You have a plan?" William Johns asked. He sounded shocked.

"Before we get into a plan, we need to evaluate the . . . ." Blackspan shook off a shudder. He removed his glasses and massaged his temples. The room remained silent. At last, he sighed. He gave instructions. "We have all the information, intelligence, endless scenarios and the like in the files we have before us. We will remain here until we formulate a plan on how to deal with this rogue nation and Russia." His rangy face was deeply worried.

A murmur of both approval and relief traveled around the table. The men began reading files and talked casually while they read.

On August 5th after careful deliberations about North Korea, the Federal Reserve and Central Intelligence Agency arrived at a solution to the PBF problem. Allan Blackspan announced, "Gentlemen." He inclined his head toward the CIA Director. "Think of our great nation as a large corporation. Like any company, if it—and our nation—is to survive, it must maintain a strong, solid currency, we must destroy the cancer that is eroding the dollar. The destruction of the Kim regime, the unification of the two Koreas, and returning the dollar to the gold standard with the vast gold reserves in northern Korea will create a behemoth banking system that will survive well into the 21st Century. Russia will be punished with lower oil prices, along with international banking sanctions. Oil will continue dropping."

"Director Perry, you will have the full, 100% support of the Obama Administration upon returning to Washington," Johns announced. "And move on your plan, Codename *KU*, for *Korea United*, immediately. A helicopter will arrive on the hour to fly you back to our beloved capital."

For an extraordinary moment, Perry became convinced the men before him ran the country. This thought gained relevance over anxiety of politics: Perry's entire purpose was going to become reality.

"God help us all," somebody murmured fervently. It was Adelman, but Perry ignored him.

Chapter 18

Craigsville

August 6, 2014

TJ could only describe the post office in Craigsville, West Virginia, as a place on the side of the road, in the middle of nowhere. For the hillbillies in the area, Craigsville was significant because it was located where the Cherry River flowed into the Gauley River. A well-kept secret was that where the two rivers met made for the best trout fishing in the United States. The locals protected this secret thoroughly, as if protecting one's own life. But a far-more valuable secret than the best fishing hole in the states was the secret facility known as the Industrial Coal Research Center, located one mile down a gravel road from the post office. The CIA chose the "coal" in the name because it neither startled nor offended anyone, coal as common to West Virginia as a dog with a bone.

Every day, except Sunday, fifteen to twenty trucks loaded with coal drove past the center, as they had for the past fifty years. The only traffic down the gravel road were the men and women that worked in the mines, or at the coal research center. Underneath the center was a TOP SECRET CIA Research Laboratory that produced spy gadgets and items needed for clandestine missions.

TJ locked the Red Robin Whiskey gift box in the trunk of the car, along with some other items he picked up at the Industrial Coal Research Center. It was not that he didn't trust the locals, but this was whiskey, a prize commodity anywhere in West Virginia. It would not be in his car long because he would give it to an old friend soon. The men driving the coal trucks tooted their loud horns and waved at TJ, who was no stranger to Craigsville. He had been coming to the area to hunt and fish for over thirty years. The late Dan Hinkle introduced TJ to the local shop owners on his first visit: "a retired Air Force Loadmaster that loves to fish!" With the blessing of eighty-four year old Dan Hinkle, TJ received immediate acceptance and never went through reappraisal. It was not that strangers were not welcome, they were just highly scrutinized.

It was half past two in the afternoon by the time Sam Young and Dave Chen finally found their way to the Craigsville Post Office. Ten minutes later TJ was fishing with his old "Osan" buddies at the mouth of the Gauley River.

Sam found himself wishing more and more strongly that he could roll back in time to when he was a boy and fished for Black Bass at a gravel pit, and say no to the Air Force recruiter that asked him to go to the Air Force Base in Niagara Falls to "check it out." The Air Force was not bad, it led him to TJ, the Federal Reserve, and where he was now in his life. But, something about fishing, and catching so many trout, made him think what life would have been like had he stayed on the farm in Appleton, New York.

He could feel the weight on his face, knowing that fishing wasn't the reason he was here.

He fell back on a large flat rock, leaned back, and closed his eyes, allowing his mind to drift into that quiet time on the farm as a boy. There was no weight on his body, or on his mind . . . Minutes passed. An hour. Finally, with a soaring burst of clarity, the words of his mother came into his head: "Korea is your destiny!"

On the banks of the Gauley River, the two Federal Reserve agents and the CIA agent sat cross-legged, like Indians, to discuss the all-important mission that they all anticipated over many years. In his midsixties, he was still "TJ the PJ" to Sam and Chen. TJ was a man of medium height and calm disposition. From his thinning hair to his hardened hands, he exuded leadership and confidence. Now, more than any time in his life, TJ knew he must use all his talents to win the two men over for the mission he was about to brief.

TJ began in his blunt style, "Sam and Dave, I think you two know better than I do the implications of the PBFs, particularly as it is tied to Putin. What it means to our economy, to our nation. And coupled with the two Malaysian airliner incidents."

Dave Chen interrupted, "I know we have a strong case against the North Koreans concerning the missing 777 out of Kuala Lumpur. Well, I just discovered a witness that can place the jet north of the 38th Parallel, at an almost exact time and date, over the Sea of Japan."

TJ and Sam both glanced at him, expressing interest. "Go on. You have our attention," TJ said.

"Yesterday, I flew on a KC-10 out of Travis AFB to McQuire. The Boom Operator, a guy named Joe Austin, is a close friend of mine. We went to the NCO Academy together at Goodfellow. The years roll by and low and behold we both go to the Senior NCO Academy together," Chen gazed over the grass to the two.

Puzzled, Sam and TJ looked at one another and back at Chen. Only Chen had an uncharacteristic way of dragging a story out. "You lost me, Chen, I don't see the connection," Sam pointed out.

TJ smiled. He was with his prized pupils and enjoyed it. Chen's matter-of-fact, emotionless voice, always carried a knockout punch. He maintained patience.

Chen shrugged, tried to smile, and looked at the two with shining eyes because he knew they were drawn to the story. "On the way to McQuire, Joe invited me into the Boom Operator Compartment to watch him refuel some F-16s. Anyways, I was curious about the long checklist boom operators carry. I always thought checklist were small and compact so they could fit in the bottom, side pocket of the flight suit. You know, like a Pararescue checklist. Joe let me examine his checklist. I saw a little drawing on a checklist page. Being a smartest, I ask Joe why he was drawing pictures on his checklist. He told me he would explain after the air-refueling. I forgot all about it until Joe mentioned it later."

"Okay, go on. We are listening," TJ said slowly.

"On March 9, 2014, Joe was refueling fighters to Misawa when he noticed a jet, a triple-seven, directly behind the KC-10, turn its anti-collision strobe and wing tip lights off. Joe thought that was the stupidest thing he ever saw a pilot do. He drew a picture of the tail-logo on his checklist. They were just passing the 38th parallel and then the jet made a hard left, toward North Korea." Chen paused thoughtfully. "The tail-logo belonged to the same airline as the missing Malaysian jet."

"Holy shit! The Malaysian airliner masked itself in the radar pattern of the KC-10 and F-16s!" TJ shrieked.

"The smoking gun. What rank is Joe?" Sam asked.

"Yes, one smoking gun. There is another one."

"It gets better," TJ said.

"To answer your question, Sam. He is a Chief Master Sergeant with over thirty years of service," Chen answered. "I thought the same thing you thought, TJ. But I wanted to back it up with facts. So I contacted a good friend of mine in Singapore, who runs the OSI Field Office there. We have a good working relationship. He launched an investigation. His investigation turned up a North Korean Spy posing as a civilian employee at ATOC (Air Traffic Operations Center). Also, there should not have been a Malaysian airliner over the Sea of Japan at nautical twilight on 9 March."

"What evidence led the OSI to the spy?" Sam asked.

"As you know, the movement of USAF fighter aircraft is classified. There was an excessive amount of 'log-ons' to the system that tracks aircraft. The OSI identified a suspect and looked into all his behavior. When they questioned him, he 'sang like a canary.' He is being held in-custody in Singapore."

"Great job, Chen. I am going to contact your friend in Singapore. This and much more will eventually get presented to Congress and the UN Security Council," said TJ in a calm, measured voice, "I just finished meeting with Mike Perry and there is a plan—a master plan to destroy the Kim regime and unify Korea. Are you ready for the details?"

For a time, Sam and Chen sat silently, their gaze fixed on TJ, awaiting what they knew was a mission briefing. The two did not answer, what they did not say carried the real meaning: *We knew this day would come.*

After giving both men a hug and the Red Robin Whiskey to Chen, TJ watched the two drive off in a Ford Explorer. He reached for the secure cell phone in his pocket. The DCIA needed to know that *KU* was in full motion.

Chapter 19

The Diplomat

August 7, 2014

If there are men destined to hell, Chul moo was at the front of the line. Over the sirens from the fire trucks, singing from a group of children, and the fluttering of 193 flags in the court yard, the FBI waited for the North Korean diplomat to exit the United Nations building.

He walked out of the building carrying a black brief case, head forward, looking from under his brows at the cameras and media. He stopped in front of the camera and removed a nuclear weapons press statement from his suit pocket.

"Mr. Kim,'" AIG (agent in-charge) Bob Turner from the New York FBI Office said.

Chul moo turned away from the camera in no great haste and looked at the agent. The agent saw the eyes change, as if he were an animal and sensed danger, to a glittery, irritated gaze. There is an emotion all psychopathic criminals process and is not named—the emotion that takes them back to their crimes. Turner was good at his job, but not good at office politics, and had it not been for 9/11 he would not be the AIG of New York. Agent Turner saw the "killer" guilt in a Chul moo's eyes. All Chul moo said was, "Yes."

Turner held out his FBI identification "I am Agent Turner from the Federal Bureau of Investigation. You are . . . ."

"The FBI," Chul Moo said, expressionless.

Turner assumed the arms akimbo position and nodded. "I am the Special Agent In-charge of the field office in New York. We need to talk with you. You need to come with us."

Chul Moo turned away from the agent toward the camera. "I want the United Nations and the people of the world to know that the United States does not agree with the North Korean position on nuclear power. Now the belligerent United States is resorting to bullying, strong arm tactics of a diplomat. I will go with the FBI to see what kind of trumped up charges they have invented. I urge freedom loving nations to file a formal protest, as my country, China, and Russia will file within the hour. Thank You." He looked around to make sure all the camera film crews were focused on him, satisfied himself that they were, and then stared toward Turner, who was looking at him with silent anticipation.

Turner leaned toward Chul moo and whispered in his ear: "I know you are a killer." Agent Turner only knew the diplomat was under suspicion for terrorist acts perpetrated on the Rainbow Bridge years ago. His job was putting the Korean diplomat in the SUV. Having spent six years as a Correction Officer at Sing Sing Prison, Turner knew men and had seen the mad eyes of killers doing multiple life sentences.

A group of agents surrounded Chul moo and led him to a waiting black GMC Yukon vehicle with tinted windows, located in the middle of a caravan of eight black suburban SUVs parked next to the concrete pillars used to stop a bomb attack. This made local television and the images quickly spread to Twitter and social media sites. The media knew the destination where the convoy was headed. Their camera crews were already set-up for the arrival of the Korean UN negotiator. The vehicles proceeded in a convoy to the Metropolitan Correctional Center (MCC), New York, United States federal administrative detention facility in Manhattan. In the past, the MCC housed high-profile criminals such as Gambino crime family boss John Gotti, Ponzi scheme man Barnard Madoff, terrorist Ramzi Yousef, and weapons trafficker Viktor Bout. What the media did not know was when the convoy became stuck in traffic in lower Manhattan, the Yukon Chul moo occupied made a right at a light, while the convoy moved straight.

The *New York Times* was permitted access to the basement of the MCC, where inmates arrived, to film the booking. Stepping out of the lead SUV, Agent Turner moved to the middle Yukon and opened the door to help the killer out of the vehicle. It occurred to Turner in less than five seconds of looking into Chul moo's eyes, I'd been thinking he was a killer—so certain of the killer trademark. And it *had* been, dammit. *Maybe I should retire. My instincts are off. This isn't a killer.*

What the media camera crew did not know was they were filming Sam Young, the identical twin brother of Chul moo, not Chul moo. After the booking, Sam Young was escorted through many channels and corridors with electronic doors at each end.

The Federal Reserve Special Tactics Unit just pulled off the biggest "switch" in modern history and many involved were not even aware what they did. These were the men that moved US currency, not in armored cars, undetected, throughout the world.

Chapter 20

California Medical Facility

August 7, 2014

The "switch" was handled with mechanical precision. Two Federal Reserve Agents, Bubby Wright and Chris Youngblood, both veteran agents of the Special Tactics Unit, dealt with Chul moo while Agent Jose Chávez drove. As soon as Chul moo got into the back of the Yukon, an agent was behind him, while another agent waited for him in the back seat. As soon as the door closed, an agent thrust a syringe into Chul moo, and he felt a burning pain in his right shoulder. His eyes flew wide open. So did his mouth. He attempted to resist by throwing his arms out to strike, but age was against him, along with the brute force from two ex-army Delta Force commandos. As the injection took its effect, he was handcuffed, blindfolded, hog-tied and restrained in a dug-out seat behind the second row of seats. A second vehicle, another Yukon, carried a team of five officers, trailed the "switch team."

"Don't you love it?" Bubby asked. "What was the injection? Damn, I wish I got to do that!"

"I don't know I was just trained to give the injection. I was told it was a watered down serum used to knock out Rhinos in the zoo. I forgot the name. He should be out of it for 8-10 hours."

They rode in silence for a while. When Buddy glanced behind the curtain he saw Chul moo lying on his back with his eyes closed—maybe dead, maybe dozing, but surely knocked out. Everything was okay as long as he was alive.

"How long you think we're going be with this prick?" Chris asked.

"I don't know. Maybe a few days, maybe a few weeks—doesn't matter, we do what we are told. Right?"

Chris didn't reply. He laced his fingers together and bent his hands backward, cracking the knuckles.

Jose grunted in agreement and concentrated on his driving, turning south onto I-95.

Flight-line security at Andrews AFB was tight. The security policeman at the ECP (entry control point) inspected the Federal Reserve Identification of the occupants and the vehicle license plate. "Are you part of VOLANT BANNER?"

"Yes sir, you bet," Jose answered.

"I never seen Federal Reserve Bank before on Presidential support missions. I was just curious. It is no problem. The Secret Service always wear little lapels on their collar. I noticed you guys don't have them. All three of you are on the access rooster."

"We are all Federal Agents and work together, sir," Jose said. He nodded his head and learned he was a sergeant. *Damn,* Jose thought, *the cop was sharp. But, then, this was the home of Air Force One, a potential target for terrorist.*

"Spot 260, a C-17," he said, looking at his clipboard again. "Tail number 20048. The Loadmaster is waiting for you."

"Thanks."

Three hundred yards away, Jose and the trail Yukon drove to the rear of the monster transport aircraft. Then came the first surprise of the day.

"Secret Service I take it," a female voice asked.

"Uh, yeah? Jose said, while all the occupants, except the two Yukon drivers, exited the vehicles.

"I'm Airman Barcelona. I'm the Loadmaster," the five foot-one Hispanic female said, extending her hand.

"Good afternoon, ma'am," he replied, shaking her hand. He was surprised such a small woman could load such a big jet.

"Okay, listen up," she said, stepping onto the Yukon floorboard. It took Airman Barcelona all of one minute to give the two drivers instructions on what she wanted done to get the Yukon into the cavern size cargo compartment.

"Welcome," a voice said, and a middle aged man in a flight suit shook hands with Bubby and Chris. "I'm Colonel Scott, the aircraft commander. We are cleared for an early departure, which means I better get in the cockpit. That is the 'rodeo champion' loading those vehicles."

"You have horses in the Air Force?" Bubby asked. He couldn't help looking at the shining full-bird rank insignia on the shoulder of the flight suit.

"No, a rodeo is an airlift competition," came the laughing reply. "She is the best C-17 Loadmaster in the Air Force. Anyways, Airman Barcelona will take care of you folks. You are welcome to visit the cockpit after we reach cruise."

After take-off, Chris placed a phone call on his secure cellphone. It took three seconds for the encryption system to work. A computerized voice said *Secure*, followed by two beeps. "Airborne," the only words he spoke into the phone. He listened to the detailed instructions. "Copy," he replied and hit the END CALL button.

Five hours later, the Special Tactics team drove into a large aircraft hangar, nicknamed the Cathedral because of large glass windows in the front of the hanger, at Travis AFB, California. The team was greeted by the senior agent from the San Francisco Federal Reserve, a large black man named Art Morris. Fifty-nine, a previous

Air Force Pararescuemen known as the black shark, he'd been with the Bank since shortly after the 9/11 attacks. Prior to 9/11, the Federal Reserve contracted out security to whatever company won the bidding process. After 9/11, the fear of an attack on the financial institution led to immediate legislation by Congress to create a new Federal Law Enforcement Agency. Within two years, the "best kept secret" in law enforcement was the highly specialized units within the Federal Reserve. Art Morris, along with Dave Chen and Sam Young, created the new police agency. No one got into a Special Tactics Unit without going through Art Morris. First of all, Art greeted all the men and offered sandwiches and juice, which they all devoured. Then came the instructions, direct and to the point. There was no time for amenities, and he wanted his subordinates to know it.

"Jose, Bubby, and Chris are part of an Asbestos Removal Company. The three of you will be operating under cover identities I have generated. The rest of you are back-up and the support team for the Korean CIA. They will be arriving at SFO in the morning," Art explained. He handed manila folders to everyone. "Your specific instructions are in the folder. Take fifteen minutes to read them. Any questions?"

"Tonight? We move again?" Bubby asked. Buddy liked Morris, and was constantly amazed by the way he masked his operational talents with humor and a show of wide-eyed innocence.

Art nodded and checked his watch. "The bed down location, California Medical Facility. You will be there shortly after 0200 hours."

Art entered the Yukon to check on Chul moo. He shined a penlight into his eyes, checked his pulse and respiration, and skin around where restraints were placed. Art watched as three men removed Chul moo from the Yukon and stuffed him into a large blue plastic barrel marked "Hazardous." The barrel was placed in the back of a white panel truck. The lettering on the box panel said ASBESTOS REMOVAL in large red letters.

"Okay, any questions?" asked Art, his smile perfunctory, for the small oxygen bottle in the barrel only lasted seventy minutes, and he wanted the men moving.

"How long will we be at this medical facility?" Chris asked.

"Make no mistake, this so called medical facility is a maximum security prison, and to answer your question: I don't know. Your folder spelled the instructions out by chapter and verse, what more do you need?" Art frowned. "I want to reiterate that no one, not even the prison warden, is aware of the subject's presence. We will keep it that way. I wish you all good luck," said the Director of Operations for the San Francisco Federal Reserve District.

It was ten minutes to two in the morning when the white panel trucked pulled into the vehicle control sally port at California Medical Facility, known as CMF, in Vacaville, California. Buddy, Chris, and Jose, stepped out of the vehicle while a correctional officer searched the vehicle. "You guys always work in the middle of the night?" The young officer asked, alternately checking the driver's license and writing their names on an entry log.

"We just finished the asbestos removal over at DVI. It is a similar joint as this, old institution. Our folks were here last week and did the asbestos in the pipe chases in the base of the towers. We are under contract with the state. This asbestos is bad shit. So we are pretty much working round the clock. We need to set-up because our folks will start tomorrow," said Bubby, smiling awkwardly.

"We do old Folsom next," said Chris.

"All right, you guys are cleared in. You will need this vehicle club on your steering wheel when you park the vehicle. The vehicle cannot stay in the institution. So after you download your equipment, one of you will have to drive it out. You can park your truck on the 'island' with the state vehicles," the officer said. He then made an announcement into his portable radio to all the towers of a vehicle entering the institution.

"I thought the perimeter fence was electrified," said Jose, "Why do you need people in the towers?"

"Good observation," the officer noted, "I probably shouldn't tell you this, but we just manned all the perimeter towers a couple hours ago. We got word that the Mexican Mafia is going to make some drug drops in the fields and orchards surrounding the institution."

"Who picks up the drugs," Jose asked.

"The minimum security inmates from our 'ranch.' Hey, we are not complaining. It is all overtime in the towers."

"Okay, how do we get to this West Sally area where we are supposed to go?" Bubby asked.

"Just drive to your left and keep going. When you get to a gate, one of you get out to hold the gate. Tower Seven will open the gate for you. Drive around the corner and an Officer will be there to help you unload and get all your equipment up to S-3. They have the area all taped off around S-3, on the third floor. He will give you keys to the unit and show you around. Then you guys are on your own."

"Thanks," Bubby said.

"All the officers and staff have been briefed to stay clear of S-3 while the asbestos removal is being done."

"Good. That makes our job easier. Bad shit. It gets in the air, you breathe a little in your lungs and . . . anyways thanks for your help," Bubby said, as the large inner gate was opened electronically by the tower officer, permitting them to enter the facility.

Chul moo awoke, in a small, white-walled cell, when he heard banging and screaming from what sounded like an area below him. The sound—some shrieking sound of horror and rage, vengeance and revenge—reminded him of the torture units at Camp 14. He laid on a concrete slab, no mattress, for a long time, contemplating where he was and assuring himself that this would not last. He raised the heels of his palms to his eyes to shield himself from the intense bright light. The air was icy-cold and then hot air with little ventilation. Getting slowly and shakily to his feet, Chul moo saw a sink and frantic thirst came to him. He stumbled to the sink but the water would not work. He tried to flush the stainless steel toilet and again nothing. He was in cell 314 on the third floor of S-Wing at California Medical Facility (CMF), also known as 'wackyville.' CMF was the largest prison in the United States for the criminally insane. Some claimed it was the biggest 'nuthouse' in the U.S. The cell had no windows, except on the door but it was covered by a metal flap. The guards opened the flap to see the position of the inmate prior to opening the door. There was a small sally port area outside the door which was entered by another door with a different key. Opposite the concrete slab was a food slot at waist level where a food tray was inserted, and where the inmate was restrained before the door was opened. The wing below him, S-2, housed psychotic inmates with the California Department of Mental Health. That scream, with nothing but killing on its mind, ripped through his brain again and again, threatening to split it and let in madness. Chul moo concluded he was in an insane asylum somewhere in the United States.

It was a lot more than just wishing he was not there; as he laid there with his hands pressed against his closed eyes, he wanted all of it to be over—he wanted back in Korea. For the first time in his fifty-five years of life, Chul moo Kim wished he could trade places with his twin brother that he had never met.

The ten other members of the "Asbestos Removal Crew" showed up the following afternoon. They were all Korean, seven men and three women, a special branch of the KCIA known as Psych Ops. Their specialty requires only they abstract information from a person and be impervious to suffering—and that is what they do and who they are. Those that have been interrogated by this team relinquished everything they wanted to know. Over time, they kept right on producing page after page of information vital to Korea, Land of the Morning Calm. Their methods included temperature control, light control, and food/water control to squeeze out the desired information. The team took advantage of highly developed medical knowledge and experience from other interrogations. After two weeks with a subject, "material rewards" were offered—more food, a mattress, or blanket. There was no consistency of methods, except for enforced sleeplessness and changing interrogators. One method the interrogators had in common, however, was they gave precedence to controlling light. The light in Chul moo's cell was extremely bright. Then when he was removed for interrogation a bright light was directed into his eyes. The first interrogations started with milder methods, and when the team intensified them, they avoided methods that left obvious marks: a broken bone or bruises. It really was not necessary to use torture in abstracting information. The team worked mainly at night, when Chul moo's normal daytime equanimity senses were off. In short, sleeplessness, lies, and threats worked best.

A masterful interrogation, KCIA Deputy Director Missy Yi thought. One of Yi's best—critical intelligence, prolific, personal, even excessive at moments. Yet the fact was, Chul moo had given them everything and more for Sam Young's mission as his double. The interrogators themselves not aware of their true purpose. Without ever telling them what was really going on, from Sam Young's private office in the basement of the New York Federal Reserve, Missy communicated with the handlers from the San Francisco Reserve. She then visited Sam, sometimes three times a day, to brief him on information gathered. She often fell asleep at his workstation, head resting on the desktop. She was wearing the same clothes as the day before.

Chapter 21

Big Boys

August 9, 2014

"I remember looking up at the balcony and watching my grandfather, the Great Leader, and Chul moo fire rounds from Block handguns into the courtyard. The gunshots did not scare me. I knew the bullets would not touch me. I was just a small boy; I dreamed of being like my grandfather," Kim Jong un, the Supreme Leader of the Democratic People's Republic of Korea, said, staring out the 10 x 10 foot window in Chongjin Villa, a 15,000 square-meter villa nestled in a valley near the northwest coastal city Chongjin. "I can imagine the greedy American puppets in Pusan are 'licking their chops' over the money on the *Green Dog*," Jong un said.

"It confirms what you have said all along, Supreme Leader," General Park, Commander of the People's Army, interjected. Park, an army general that escaped the recent 'purge,' the killing of over 200 top-level government and military leaders, when Kim Jong un assumed power. "The Americans are making a big mistake if they are 'pulling the strings' on the seizure of the *Green Dog*."

"Why is that general? And do you think the *Green Dog* is related to my uncle's detention in New York?" Kim Jong un asked, his back turned on the general as he looked out the window. *It was in this very room, while I played below, that my grandfather anointed Chul Moo his son*, Jong un could not help thinking.

"First of all, Supreme Leader, I want to commend you on your leadership skills at a time of crisis. I was a captain under your grandfather, Kim Il sung, the Great Leader, and you are very much like him. You do not show weakness and your decision of not being content to play defense is a brilliant move on your part. On your request, I have ordered 3 divisions toward the DMZ, activated our mini-subs, and put the entire People's military on high-alert. We are prepared to wipe the cowards out once and for all."

"Of course, of course, General. Answer my question!" Kim Jong un shouted. The thick, oval face and heavy build of Kim Jong un became exaggerated when he lost his temper.

"Question?" Park replied, becoming a tad woozy around the edges.

Kim Jong un turned around from the window, his frightening vacant eyes on the general. "Why are the Americans making a mistake and is the *Green Dog* related to my uncle's detention!" he repeated, those terrible eyes of his never leaving the general.

"Well . . . the Americans have Putin and the Chinese to contend with . . . I believe the *Green Dog* and the New York detention are related. It is obvious the United States is muscling its power because it did not get what it wanted at the recent UN talks over our nuclear power ambitions. The key to his release is the condemnation of Russia and

China. They both have filed protest and, together, they will secure his release." Park stopped talking and bowed at the waist.

Something in Park's voice caught the Supreme Leader's attention, and he squinted his eyes to take a closer look at him. Kim Jong un glanced at his bodyguards, then toward General Park. It was a quick glance, really no more than a flick, but the bodyguards had seen it more than once, and it was a death sentence upon the general.

"Take him away! He is a traitor!" Kim Jong un said with perfect assurance, "and the rest of you sit down at the table."

"No! You are making a mistake!" Park cried in a shrill voice. But the old man only drew the bodyguards closely around him as they drought him out of the room, his eyes looked to the First Secretary of the Workers' Party and the Chairman of the Central Military Commission. "Tell him!" Park said, still looking at his Party colleagues. Years earlier, they were fellow crooks together in Pyongyang, stealing money right under Kim Jong il's nose.

The men did not look at Park, did not stir, and then sat down at a circular table.

Kim Jong un moved with a limp toward the table and sat down; he removed a stick of Swiss cheese from his pocket, unwrapped it, and began chewing it. He swallowed hard, squinting against the revulsion he felt, then aware the two men saw it. They averted their eyes from the fiery Supreme Leader. Kim sighed with frustration, thinking, as he often did, that he needed to upgrade his submarines. He sat upright in a straight chair, hovering like a giant bird of prey that just ate a mouse. "What is your take on this 'act' by the bitch government in the south and the pig Americans?"

"I am impressed by your dedication to our country and your response, Supreme Leader," the first secretary said, "these actions will surely anger Russia, our true friend, China, and our supporters around the world."

"They are cowards, Supreme Leader, absolute cowards," the chairman snapped. "We'll get an update from our undercover operatives around Pusan. And I suspect Putin will employ his resources. He is very powerful and feared by the American 'monkey' president, as well as the Europeans. Putin has all of Europe 'on the ropes' over Ukraine."

"There is no doubt---to my mind at least--- that this is some sort of plot concocted by the Americans, Japanese, and the whore in the south. I refer to the whore Yi in the KCIA, not the whore president. A plot to steal the $15 billion destined to Putin," the first secretary said, nodding his head.

The chairman pondered. "An FSB agent was found dead in Kuala Lumpur. The same place the *Green Dog* originated. No doubt connected to this mess. The Japanese are like rats in Malaysian, the 'economic rodents' they are." The chairman was not in the loop of whatever exactly happened to the missing Malaysian Airliner. He was taking a risk just saying Kuala Lumpur.

Kim Jong un sat for a moment nodding, his mind somewhere else. The mention of Kuala Lumpur caused him to have a momentary unsettling thought: *maybe this is all related to "The Great Hijacking."*

The first secretary nearly exploded. "When talking about the Americans, the Japanese, and the whore south, nothing's impossible. We will destroy them!"

Kim Jong un listened intently, pulled out a pack of Marlboro cigarettes, and lit one, the signal for the other two to do so as well. A sense of relief traveled between the two party officials.

For a moment, Kim Jong un did not move but merely sucked in the cigarette. His features seemed to melt with each inhalation, finally his jaw clamped tight. "I propose that we communicate with Russia and China on this issue. We go about as if nothing happened, with the exception of positioning of our forces, especially our mini-subs. What is the American military up to in Osan?"

As the Supreme Leader enunciated the last words a gunshot erupted from the courtyard below. Kim Jong un grinned. He remembered the *Godfather* movies he watched with his father when he was growing up. *I am the Godfather*, he thought.

The room instantly was silent.

Kim Jong un blinked and glanced around the silent room that was essentially the same as when his grandfather was alive. He studied the men's faces, looking for signs of guilt. "Well what do you think?"

Color slowly returned to the two pale faces as they nodded their approval.

"Brilliant, Supreme Leader, brilliant! It is not what they expect," the chairman exclaimed, although his voice did not sound hopeful. For Chairman Chang, the hard part was keeping an impassive face. He had to pretend that everything Kim Jong un said was of extreme importance, when he'd much prefer to escape out of the country. But he couldn't do that. He had to think of his family. He needed to change the subject to something the Supreme Leader loved—like Basketball. "The upcoming exhibition game with Red Robin will attract the Western media."

For his part, Secretary Ling felt his heart not so much skip a beat as stop entirely for about five seconds, so it seemed. "The Americans are staging a huge airlift with C-17s from Travis AFB. It is somewhat of a response to our activity along the DMZ. They do not take us seriously, Supreme Leader," Ling said. He kept his eyes on Kim . . . but with an effort.

Startled, Kim Jong un cast another glance at Ling. "Why do you say that?"

"Because our agents in Osan report the C-17s are loaded with outdated MREs, their equivalent to meals for soldiers in the field. They are selling the MREs at a discount to the south just to get rid of them. If they viewed our actions seriously, the planes would be loaded with troops. They want to give the appearance of responding to our actions," Ling concluded.

The Supreme Leader did not dispute Ling's analysis. "I like your attention to details, Ling. What about China and Russia?" All of his intellect was being required to keep his grip on power in face of the *Green Dog* crisis. He could not allow his bad judgment to show like it did over the recent release of a silly Hollywood movie.

"Yes, the 'Big Boys,' Russia and China," he had to say in reply, as soon as he got breath back in his lungs. "Let them deal with the weak American President." But Ling thought that was what the Supreme Leader wanted to hear after his recent international computer hacking disaster over a newly released comedy about North Korea, an incident that was far more frightening to Ling than the present crisis.

"Oh, the 'Big Boys,' Putin and the Chinese. We will see who our friends are," the Supreme Leader said in surprise, and waved his hands up as if to signify the matter resolved. "The Red Robin visit will be perfect. I look forward to seeing my good friend." He turned, quick as a snake, toward the balcony window. Out of the corner of his eye he saw a portrait of the Great Leader hanging on the wall--reviving a pleasant memory of his youth. He dragged on his Marlboro, coughed out smoke and looked at the two old men. "Go, go! Get out of here!"

Rattled as they were, it only took the men a few seconds to leave the room, bowing as they left.

Chang and Ling were gone only a few minutes when Kim Jong un was drawn back to the balcony window. It occurred that less than fifteen minutes ago, he'd been thinking of playing as a child—so perfect to be inspired by the Great Leader himself! He had a momentary unsettling thought: *maybe Chul moo's detention was tied into a plot to kill him. No, enemies are always within Korea, not from the outside. He must get Chul moo back. He was the only man he could trust. He supposed he had known at least that much, but it wasn't until now that he realized how he depended on him. Where did things go wrong?*

No answers came, only the irrational but powerful voice of his mother telling him how he would grow up and become a great leader. He was supposed to be the Supreme Leader for the rest of his life. And, bizarre as it sounds, the thought calmed him down.

No, he could not relax until Chul moo was back. At least not yet.

Chapter 22

Game On

August 11, 2014

Chen, wearing a TSA uniform, watched Billy Becker, aka Red Robin, through the security Plexiglas, from his position, next to an image scanner at customs and immigration at San Francisco International Airport. Wearing a Chicago Bulls jersey, along with shorts and untied high-top basketball shoes, and with a Douglas MacArthur corncob pipe dangling from the corner of his mouth, Billy stopped briefly for the camera crews and to answer a few questions.

"I don't care what the State Department says," Billy repeated for the third time. He removed the pipe, tilted his sunglasses down toward his nose ring, and looked into the camera. "Kim Jong un is my friend, he is a good man, and I love him. He is my friend. I don't care what the government says. He is my friend."

"Do you realize the United States does not sanction your visit?" the channel 40 news anchor asked.

"Fuck them punks! They can sanction this!" Billy said, while grapping his groin. "I take that back. What I mean to say is it is better to talk basketball than not to talk at all, call it 'basketball diplomacy.' I am going to spend my entire time with my friend. I'll talk to you guys when I get back," Billy said with great relish, as if he now was a seasoned ambassador. He put the unlit pipe back in his mouth and pushed through the cameras toward the security screening.

The San Francisco crowd burst out clapping. The Red Robin visit tickled them more than the Occupy Wall Street protests.

The media drama over, Becker passed through the metal detector and moved to the end of the roller conveyers at the end of the image detector, where he collected his duffle bag and Red Robin Whiskey gift box. Neither Billy, or, so it seemed, the new TSA Officers, knew what had just happened: the Red Robin Whiskey gift box was switched with what looked like an exact duplicate gift box. The privileged Japanese businessmen looked on with disdain from their security line because the basketball Hall of Fame player did not even have to take his size 12 shoes off or remove his sunglasses. The champion rebounder attributed his smooth transition through the TSA screeners as his rite of passage bestowed by the government for his "diplomatic role" he played in fostering relations with North Korea. Becker glanced over his shoulder, nodded at the gawkers, then turned into the first bar for a few drinks. Billy B. Becker had a reservation on the 11:30 plane to Beijing with a connecting flight to Pyongyang.

The Pyongyang Indoor Stadium included four basketball courts, a swimming pool, various gymnastic rooms, and a huge hall, recently remodeled by the Supreme Leader himself, displaying photographs of Kim Jong un playing various sports, but mainly basketball. Ninety-percent of Pyongyang was destroyed during the Korean War. After the war, the city was rebuilt with Soviet aid. Kim Il sung modeled the city after Moscow, with many of the buildings constructed in the style of Socialist Classicism. Below the Indoor Stadium is a sub-basement level which allows DPRK leadership easy access to attend events at the stadium from the Central Committee buildings. A secret underground passageway under the stadium existed, connected to a vast labyrinth of escape tunnels, build like a maze—to confuse users, except the Supreme Leader. As a boy, Jong un moved through the tunnels with his grandfather, who often killed the secret light switch and left Jong un behind in the dark. It was a rite. He had the longest, quietest, darkest walk imaginable; he developed a unique way of concentrating. But it was Kim Il sung's paranoia, along with the influence of men like Laurenti Beria and Joseph Stalin, which influenced Kim's thinking on the design for the center of his new capital. Kim's fear of the city being bombed, his regime imploding, and assassination led him to design escape tunnels and underground shelters. And he learned from the masters of terror—Beria and Stalin.

At the 13 August opening ceremony of the Exhibition Game, a crowd of 14,000 all clapped in unison after Billy Becker sang a verse from the Michael Jackson song, *Behind the Mask,* to Kim Jong un, who was seated above in the stands. At the completion of his atrocious singing, Billy looked up at Kim un, dedicated the game to him, and then bowed deeply at the waist. The crowd clapped again. To the other American NBA players that accompanied Billy the crowd looked as if they had been brainwashed in an institution, sent on the grim task to watch a game they knew nothing about, and clap on cue. They *had*.

Billy played in the first half of the game with the other Americans. The Koreans were ahead 47-39 at half-time. The Americans were split up for the second half, mixed in with Korean team. Billy did not play, but sat next to Kim Jong un and his wife in the stands for the second half of the exhibition. His gift, the Red Robin whiskey, the sole decoration, displayed on a table in front of Kim. The Supreme Leader's mind began to drift during the second half of the game, as if hypnotized with a kind of bemused wonder by the Red Robin. His wife's eyes quivered in dismay by Billy's outward show of affection for her, but it was Kim's helpless curiosity—it was the expression, she was quite sure, that he would send her to another mansion, not Ryongsong Residence, while her husband engaged in a conference of upmost importance. Her role was to obey and honor the Supreme Leader.

Through the open window, the scent of the Siebold Magnolia, the national flower, floated in from the lush garden at Ryongsong, as Kim Jong un mingled with five naked girls in a large circular bed. The same bed the Great Leader used to sleep in with multiple young girls. He believed that rolling around in bed with many young women prolonged his life span and kept him strong. The grandson thought it a great tradition and had no intention of ever abandoning such wisdom handed down from the Great Leader. He instructed one of the girls to pour some more Red Robin. She rushed out of bed to prepare the drink.

Kim stumbled out of bed and saw Sook, his favorite concubine, bowed at the waist and with both hands extended, she held the glass. He passed her and moved to the balcony to view the lighted garden. He noticed a ghostly glimmer of black color to the Kimilsungia and Kimjongilia, the orchids cross-bred and named after his grandfather and father. *The flower that blooms around the world for the Kim's love and praise*, thought Kim Jong un. He suddenly felt a pain in his stomach. He felt exhausted. Moving to grab the balcony, his vision blurred, and the black flowers brought a deeper chill; it was as if the metaphor his mind seized upon had become real. The inheritor of the Kim regime missed the hold on the balcony and like a rocket hitting its intended target, he landed in the flowers of evil, a dead man.

Chapter 23

Ambassadors

September 2, 2014

The mood in the UN Security Council Chamber was tense. Permanent members Russia and China led the discussions and insisted on the release of Chul moo Kim or risk a possible military confrontation on the Korean peninsula. It did not facilitate matters that it was the month the Russia Federation assumed the role as President of the UN Security Council. Kim Jong un had not been seen in public for close to two weeks. The rumors of a palace coup, surgery in Switzerland, and secret travel to China circulated through the media. The strongest rumor was he was in an underground bunker planning for war. The United States discussed, sometimes heatedly, the evidence of terrorism and counterfeit US currency against the Office 39 Director. Russia pointed out the lawlessness of South Korea in seizure of the *Green Dog* and linked the event to Chul moo's detention. Despite the objection of the United States, the Security Council wanted a vote on a resolution. Because the U.S. was a party to the dispute it abstained from the vote. U.S. Ambassador Yeva Schur tried to attach a rider to the resolution that would prevent Chul moo Kim from ever holding a political position within North Korea.

Ambassador Victor Cherniss announced, "Resolution 3298, the release of Chul moo Kim and the end to the *Green Dog* Quarantine passes!" He blinked and took a long breath. "I want to thank all fifteen members on a quick and unanimous vote on the rule of law, the compliance with obligations under the United Nations Charter."

They were alone in a room adjacent to the Security Council Chamber, the Russian and American Ambassador. Yeva Schur requested the meeting, and the Russian Ambassador had thought it best to talk where no one else could hear them. The bond between the two ambassadors was their shared profession. And that was all it was. Cherniss was "old school" KGB, a protégé of Vladimir Putin, who in years past had flown the Soviet Flag in some favorite hot spots, among them Berlin and Warsaw. Like a Hollywood actor, Cherniss didn't so much have to be intelligent as to play the intelligent diplomat.

"Oh Yeva, yes, good evening," he said as soon as Schur appeared. "I knew you would show up to exchange barbs!"

Yeva knew the Ambassador's prevarications inside out. In a minute he would tell her she is out of her league and should return to banking.

"Where is Kim Jong un?" Yeva began, as soon as she sat down.

"Ambassador Schur, your attempt to attach riders to the resolution was ludicrous!" Russian Ambassador Victor Cherniss snapped. "How would we know where he is? He is a lone wolf."

"He is a thug and in bed with Putin. You know that as well as I do."

"Yeva, Yeva, the Russian in you is showing its colors. Honestly, we . . ."

"Don't feed me your shit. I am not Russian. I was born in Ukraine and am an American!"

"You went to school at the National Pedagogical University in Kiev, a Russian school. Yeva," said Cherniss, as if talking to his daughter. "We do not have a clue as to his whereabouts. I was going to ask you the same question. I think he is in a bunker plotting mayhem. Your airlift on the peninsula has him worried, I am sure."

"Okay, I believe you. I take that back about him and Putin. Putin barely knows Jong un. It is Putin and Chul moo that are 'birds of a feather.' The two are both thugs and partners in crime."

"You wanna know what I think? I think you're pissed because we got the upper hand on getting Chul moo out of Rikers Island. And watch what you say about Putin. He is the most powerful, popular man on the earth at the moment."

Yeva chuckled.

"No, I'm serious," said Cherniss. "Putin will have an Aeroflot jet on the tarmac in two hours to pick Chul moo up. It is over the pole and back to Pyongyang for him. I'm sure Kim Jong un will emerge when his big uncle shows up."

"He is not at Rikers Island. Listen carefully Ambassador. We know you had your 'fingers in the fire' concerning the two Malaysian jets. It is going to cost you. The sanctions are going to increase. How do you feel Ambassador?" She asked it the way you ask a sick person.

"Wonderful!" said Cherniss, with a morose smile. "Do you speak for the President or have you gone 'rogue.' Because the Obama Administration is all talk. In fact, Ambassador, I think you are out of your league and should go back to work for the Federal Reserve Bank. This entire Korean crisis is over your head. Stick to Ukraine. The Baltics. Your area of expertise."

She had him. He was staggered. The dimensions of Russian involvement once more hogged the moral terrain. "Oil? We will keep the price of oil low for some time. The *Green Dog* will leave Pusan but will not port in Vladivostok."

"Where will it port?"

Yeva nodded, all the while studying his face and noting, with satisfaction, that he remained stunned. "The ship will depart Pusan in accordance with the UN Resolution."

The Russian Ambassador's nostrils quivered, and his jaw muscles bunched up, as if he were trying to keep from retching. "How is your lovely twin sister, Olena Loboda? Where is she? We know she visited Boris Nemtsov. Is she off looking for a Jewish husband like yours, or is she on a research ship chasing a Great Blue Whale!"

Yeva stared at him for what seemed like a very long time, then opened her mouth and closed it, as if rejecting the usual response of surprise or disbelief when a disaster is announced. What she finally said, while perfectly logical, puzzled Cherniss: "Kodiak, Alaska, researching Salmon migration. Why?"

"Well, reckless engagements for one. Nemtsov is a thorn in our side with his 'movement' and so-called pamphlet." *Oh, he had stunned her, all right, and clearly knocked the condescending look off her face,* he thought, *and how contemptible a strategy it was . . . . But perhaps a mistake to reveal his hand.*

"If anything happens to my sister or Nemtsov, I will hold you . . ."

"Now you sound more like the Obama Administration, making threats with nothing to back it up. Why we hack into the White House emails and your President does nothing. Oh, excuse me, he does shake his finger at Putin."

"Ukraine is Putin's downfall if he stays on the course he has chartered."

"Yeva—do you know what I was taught in college about Ukraine?" He studied her face to see if by any chance she was listening. A blank. She was thinking about her sister. He plunged on.

"Russia without Ukraine is a country. Russia with Ukraine is an Empire!"

With great seriousness she looked into his eyes and said:

"Times have changed. Ukraine and Nemtsov will bring Putin down, he will not have enough riot police to stop the protests and demonstrations." Yeva's tone gave nothing away. It was flat, without expression. The face said nothing either, and the eyes seemed slightly shrouded as if they stared only into their own private world. "Cherniss, there are no empires any longer!"

"I will pass on your regards to Putin . . . ." The Russian Ambassador glanced toward the door and then lowered his voice. "It is always a pleasure, Yeva."

She preferred not to say what was on her tongue.

Yeva stood by the flags outside of the UN, the same spot that Chul moo gave his speech weeks before, for a long undecided moment, wishing she could clear the fog over the location of her identical twin sister. Olena, a marine biologist, went out to sea often on research projects. But even then she maintained contact with her. She was certain that Olena was safe. The two of them processed a kind of twin telepathy. Olena injured her hand when she was a student at the Institute of Marine Sciences, and Yeva immediately knew something was wrong. The mystery as to why she did not return phone calls and emails became clearer now. She seemed to wink out of existence like a soap bubble. Now the FSB was looking for her. The "Kodiak" story was merely that, a story to send the FSB off into the Alaskan wilderness. She remembered the quick, appraising look, and expression of relief creep into Cherniss' eyes when she told him. Yeva was crying. She pulled a mirror from her purse to get mascara out of her eye. Looking in the mirror she saw what she knew was Olena's facial expression for what it really was: terror.

Chapter 24

Return to Pyongyang

September 13, 2014

At ten past ten, a chartered jet from the Aeroflot Fleet, a Boeing 737-800, named V.Belinsky after the Russian literary critic, took off from LaGuardia Airport. Sam Young—assuming the identity of his identical twin brother—watched the plane fly over New York City. The aircraft leveled off at a cruise altitude of 38,000 feet, and a senior FSB major and an aide of Chul moo's moved across the table from Sam to brief him on current events on the peninsula. The passenger area looked like a miniature version of an office lounge. For a long moment Sam and the Russian regarded each other from their opposite ends of the table, seeing each other perfectly well in spite of the deepening differences and two feet that separated them. The major was young for his rank, a sign of further promotion if this assignment went well.

"Pass on to Vladimir Putin my upmost gratitude in his work helping to ensure my release," Sam said in English. "You must excuse me. My Russian is weak at the moment."

"I understand. There was a process in securing your release," the major replied in passable English. "Russia played the key role in your release," the major told him.

"Inform President Putin that there is a major crisis, a sort of shake-up, within my government, but assure him that I will resolve it and will contact him directly in the days to come."

"Indeed?" The major wasn't taken aback, but he became instantly wary. He wanted to know details, but suspected Chul moo did not trust him. Nobody really trusts anybody else. "What will it mean to our country?"

"The relationship between Korea and Russia will only grow stronger. I have something that is the salvation for us both—unlimited greenbacks and gold. That will be all, thank you. I wish to speak with my aide in private," Sam said, turning his head, dismissing the major, who rose from his seat and moved toward the rear of the empty jet.

"Tell me in your words what the *hell* is going on?" demanded Young, the double, obviously not surprised as he accepted his aide, Jin Lee's presence. "Good to see you Lee. I know you can be trusted."

"I apologize, Director. It's been a difficult time . . . not talking to you in such a confusing time."

For the next fifteen minutes Sam Young listened to the disturbing doubts of Lee as to whom was running the government in North Korea. He feared making an analysis of the situation—the question of who was alive and who was dead—not knowing himself if the Supreme Leader was in-fact alive. Lee feared his boss, Chul moo, more than anyone, but the detention seemed to have softened him.

"I believe the Supreme Leader is dead. I received information of a possible plot to murder Kim Jong un just hours before I was detained. The connection to our Leader's disappearance and my subsequent detention is all too obvious. Coupled with the plot I uncovered, the absence of the Supreme Leader, and the various power struggles and shootings, there can be no doubt Kim Jong un is dead," Sam lowered his head, his face contorted in agony.

"Ah!" whispered Lee. "Is it *possible*? The Supreme Leader dead? Why?"

"As you know, a goal of the Great Leader himself, Kim Il sung has always been the unification of Korea. The Supreme Leader formulated a plan with the south to tear down the DMZ and unite the two countries under his leadership. A plan very similar to Germany's unification plan. The plan would have unified the peninsula without a shot being fired. When the hardliners within the government discovered information of the plan they gunned our leader down like a dog. The Americans want the status quo because of the so-called military industrial complex. They detained me. Had it not been for Vladimir Putin, I would still be in jail or dead."

Jin Lee started to view the meeting as divine, for he began to grasp that Chul moo was now the Kim that ruled the nation. Lee closed his eyes and tried to deny what sat before him. He assumed he was hallucinating and was, himself, now the aide to the leader of his country. But when he opened his eyes, Chul moo was still there. His voice was level and controlled, as if it was actually possible, at least at this point, to ask the question. "What do I call you? What divine name will you use?"

Realizing what Lee was asking him, Sam was thinking very fast, running through the possibilities. He closed his eyes and saw the vision of his mother before him telling him, *Korea is your destiny.* He removed a piece of blank paper from his brief case and wrote Destiny in Hangul characters. He slid the note to Lee.

Lee stared at the paper. "Very good, Destiny. Very good." Lee paused, looking intently at Sam Young.

"I will name you vice-chairman of the NDC (National Defense Commission). The most important and critical work is before us at this moment, a serious of events that must occur before this plane lands on the tarmac at Pyongyang," the double said, then added wryly, "If not executed properly, we will be gunned down within minutes of our arrival."

"You've got my full attention," Lee said.

Sam pulled a sheet of paper from the folder at his elbow and slid it across the small table. The paper showed a Janggi (Korean Chess) board with some pieces circled. "I believe you know what the circles mean. We discussed the plan the last time we played. If I remember right, you won the game," Sam said.

"Destiny, I can never beat you again. You are too wise," Lee replied.

"Nonsense. You are a great strategist and the best public relations man on the peninsula. Now, the 'General' and 'Chariots' that are circled, you understand the prearranged plan and code names," Sam said sternly. "Are you listening?"

"Of course. I can see the circles and understand the strategy."

"The 'General' and 'Chariots' must be removed from the 'board' before we land in Anchorage to refuel. You know the code word to give my private army to make this happen. This aircraft is equipped with a secure HF radio and email capability. Tell the Russian FSB agent you have an important message that must be passed to the Supreme Leader. Only a handful of people know the code.

Lee nodded. "What about the 'elephants' and 'guards' that are circled? This plan is eliminating the ruling elite. The ruling elite will take all available measures to ensure state survival—state survival equals their survival, and perhaps ours?"

Sam blinked his eyes and looked at him. "We will make secure phone calls from the Air Force Command Post at Elmendorf AFB. That will launch the second phase with the 'guards' and 'elephants.' I know that expression. What happening in your head?"

Lee didn't reply but shook his head absently. "The Janggi Board on the paper is the Chinese Board but it is missing the Xianggi River that divides the board. And the Americans will never let us in their secure communications post," Lee said.

"Good observation. We are playing a new game now. Nothing divides the board, no River, no DMZ. The strategy is unification of Korea! Tell the Russian he must arrange secure communication from the Air Force Base or he will be shot!"

Wary of not obeying orders, Lee moved to the rear of the aircraft to speak with the FSB agent. From across the passenger compartment, the double caught the FSB agent's eye. Sam made a gesture toward the cockpit door and a minutes later, Lee was escorted into the cockpit of the 737-800, V. Belinsky.

It was late in the afternoon when the V. Belinsky landed in Anchorage. The Ted Stevens Anchorage International Airport shared Runway 63 with the Air Force at Elmendorf AFB. An Air Force "Follow Me" truck led the aircraft to a parking spot in front of Base Operations. Sam and Lee were escorted by six armed security policemen, past a Kodiak Bear mounted in a glass case in the AMC (Air Mobility Command) Passenger Terminal, to the Elmendorf Command Post. The passenger terminal and corridors were entirely empty. A door buzzed open and they were in the Elmendorf Command Post.

The customary hubbub of activity of the command post was absent. The room was dark. All of the computers had been turned off and covered with plastic, with the exception of one computer, the bizarre screen saver shooting streaks of lights across the desk. Sam walked toward the light in the large room. An airman was sitting at the desk, reading the Stars and Stripes. He looked up when he saw the two Koreans.

"You can use this computer," Airman Monges said. "The keyboard is in Korean and the computer is encrypted. It will self-destruct twenty minutes after I log on for you."

"Fine," Sam said, and nodded for Lee to sit down.

The airman walked away from the two.

Lee began typing away. Nothing existed for him except the computer screen before him and twenty minutes.

Sam Young, the brother of the devil Chul moo, thought of the 737-800 as a giant teleport vehicle delivering him to unchartered territory, full of unexpected dangers. Nevertheless, Sam always felt connected in some mysterious way to the clouds of evil over North Korea and conceded his own dark clouds looked like a light mist compared to the dark clouds under the Kim regime. By the time the aircraft reached cruise, Sam estimated the toll from the killing machine exceeded 400. Sam, once the knight in shining armor, now hideous, as he reeked of the death of hundreds.

"They would have killed us," the double said, sounding like Chul moo. The only option was death—the power struggle is over. By eliminating enemies, I took away their motive. Our options were clear: we could have taken on the hardliners and eventually gotten killed, or we could eliminate opposition. In the end, eliminating opposition saved our lives."

"Yes, Destiny," Lee said, bowing his head. Lee felt unclean and unsure. But he knew Chul moo was right: it should be over. It would just take time for things to return to normal again. It was the normalcy that scared Lee. For a few instances, he thought Chul moo changed from the detention, he seemed softer, more benevolent. But as a movie screen played in his head, Lee saw all the executions, all the bullets to the back of the head. The only comparison Lee could think of in regards to Chul moo's private army was the Gestapo of Nazi Germany. Yes, the killings, the camps, and the brutality would continue as a normal everyday event in Korea because a Kim still ran the county. A fear began to swell inside Lee, and he could not help wandering if Chul moo was paving the road to his own downfall and releasing a tidal wave of blood that would soon surge throughout the most inner workings of the government. Korea would never change.

For Koreans, whose defense against Chul moo's forces failed, and the many government officials suffering casualties, the rise of Chul moo was the beginning of the end for the Kim regime. The purges by Chul moo became a turning point of a different sort. What happened within the farms and cities stiffened Korean determination to expel the Kim regime. No doubt, the twelve hours, while the double was enroute to Pyongyang, Chul moo's police forces were marked by countless incidents of almost indescribable ruthlessness. The cities and villages found themselves "under the gun" of the Kim regime. Ironically, those that witnessed the horror managed to send word to the outside world. In the rise of Chul moo, the killings were concentrated within twelve hours, mostly in the night.

Sam Young, the gladiator, stepped off the 737 onto red carpet, flowers, and an array of singing children. Pyongyang was under martial law and the size of the military at the airport clearly demonstrated Sam Young was in-charge. For the first time since stepping on North Korean soil, Sam, wearing his customary Block 19 and Block 21 handgun on each hip, turned to Lee and asked a question. His voice was firm and intelligent.

"I have changed my mind, we will not go to my mansion in Sinuiju. Instead, we will stay in Pyongyang at the Ryongsong Residence," Sam ordered.

Lee ducked his head in a quaint little bow. "Yes, I will inform the soldiers."

"Inform the information crew to film one statement for broadcast to the nation," Sam said.

When the state media crew was set up, Sam stepped into the thongs of the children. Surrounded by ten-year olds, Sam stated the thesis that would begin to move the nation.

"The goal of the Great Father, Kim Il sung, has always been the unification of the two Koreas. Sooner not later," he stated, "the two Koreas will unite as one nation!" After making the statement, Sam moved toward an armored GAZ all-terrain vehicle, instead of the customary Mercedes.

A stunned silence greeted his statement, to which Lee's own amazement contributed. Nowhere, in the arrival instructions on the aircraft, had Lee been briefed on the changes. A fresh clamor emerged throughout the country.

At the Ryongsong Residence, in northern Pyongyang, Sam surprised everyone when he made his unannounced visit, the workers were taking a mid-afternoon break in the courtyard within the 4½ square mile complex surrounded by a lethal electric fence and mine fields. Sam stepped through the front door, removed his shoes, and entered a huge living room. He heard a low cough and saw the head butler.

"I want you to give me a tour," his voice roared out at him, making him leap back in fear, all the while maintaining his low bow.

Sam took a pack of Marlboros from his breast pocket and shook one out for the old butler. "You can smoke it later, outside," Sam said. "Do you know how to get to the underground tunnels?"

"Not exactly. But I can get you to the hideout locations. You will need a passcode to enter. The hideout locations are ingenious!"

"Very well. Lead the way."

About the same time that Sam was getting the mansion tour. Lee was meeting with both the Supreme People's Assembly (SPA) and the members of the Workers' Party of Korea. By unanimous decision, Chul moo was confirmed as the 4th Supreme Leader of North Korea. The news went out over the wires that Kim Jong un had died of an aneurysm and his uncle was now the leader of the most closed, secretive society in existence. The body of Kim Jong un would be placed on a raised podium in Juche Square the following day, and the new leader Kim Chul moo would made a speech.

Chapter 25

Juche Square

September 15th, 2014

A great crowd filled Juche Square and the mood appeared somber. All eyes turned to Sam as he stood on a stage in front of the Juche Tower, Kim Jong un's casket was before him on a raised podium surrounded by glass. Kimilsungia and Kimjongilia adorned the casket.

"It has always been an insatiable desire of the Great Father for the two Koreas to be unified. In 1989, almost twenty-five years ago, the Berlin Wall came down. This led to cracks in the communist system. Communism in Russia and China changed more toward a free market. We in Korea see the benefits of free market with the Black Market and illegal trade across the border with China. A wave of change has swept throughout the world. The Supreme Leader recognized this from his travels and education abroad. Kim Jong un's compulsion, one that set him apart from his father and grandfather, was his insatiable desire to set the country on a new path. He concluded talks on the day of his death with the South for convoys of food to cross the border into our country. Nothing pained the Supreme Leader more than the famines and lack of food within the country. In honor of his death and in keeping the agreement with Kim Jong un, the South will begin delivering convoys of food tomorrow. This arrangement was conducted between the two Koreas and is a huge humanitarian package. Also, tomorrow the Dali Lama will arrive to pay his respects to the Supreme Leader."

Sam saw the eyes wide open and hands over the mouths of many in the crowd. All state speeches were cover-ups and lies, along with justifications told and retold. They had never heard the truth before and was shocked. There was absolutely no noise as he spoke. He continued.

"There is no reason in the era we live in that people exactly alike are divided by barb wire and a DMZ. I will do my best to cleanse the nation of the past. In years to come, the division of our peninsula will be a mere blip in history. I must go to coordinate further activities. Pay your respects to the Supreme Leader." Sam's eyes were misty as he considered the enormity of the speech's meaning and what would happen. He turned and exited the stage, stepping into a black Mercedes stretch that drove him back to Ryongsong Mansion.

At Ryongsong, Sam used a Russian speaker, whose voice sounded like Chul moo's, from the Spy School, to talk with Vladimir Putin. In the breaking of the convoy and Dali Lama news there was no transition. Putin, having witnessed the speed of the fall of the Berlin Wall and collapse of the Soviet Union, stressed for Chul moo to maintain the status quo. As a cushion, the voice of Chul moo reiterated he would secure the release of the *Green Dog*, anchored in the Yellow Sea, west of Seoul, and soon the flow of PBFs would resume.

Chapter 26

UN Security Council

September 27, 2014

Ambassador Victor Cherniss flattened himself against the leather armchair, leaned back, feeling the sweat run down his back, his eyes seeing somewhere faraway in both space and time. His blood temperature dropped another degree or so. Russia had not risk anything of consequence—oh, yes, they risk a huge supply of counterfeit currency and gold should North Korea's leadership change hands, but that is something they did not talk about. The situation on the Korean peninsula reminded him in many ways of Berlin. The suddenness with which change came. In the autumn of 1989, people were machine gunned to death while attempting to go over the wall. In November of the same year people were tearing the wall down with pick axes and hammers. The wave of change had begun with Kim Jong un's death, and though in the past, change had been successfully put down with brutal force by the Kim regime, this time the brutal force was used against the ruling elite. The speech by the Dali Lama with calls to move forward toward freedom and openness acted like a spark among the youth. The Dali Lama proved to be a leader that could unite Koreans with his words of hope. Buddhism was introduced in 372 AD and provided the ideological backing for the Kingdom of Koguryo. The Dali Lama reinvigorated Buddhism to the faith starved Koreans, so influential were his words in bringing attention to freedom that the Chinese Government, fearing its power, conspired to ban him in China. The convoys of food filled the bellies of every North Korean. That was it: feed a starving people. Cherniss inhaled deeply, repeatedly, to regain his focus to the task at hand in the UN Security Council Chamber.

"Ok, we have attended multiple meetings, scenario studies, functional task groups, and have as the Americans say, 'beat the horse to death.' What are the concerns on the table?"

"I believe Russia shares China's view of seeing this crisis contained within North Korea itself to prevent an international crisis," Chinese Ambassador Choi said.

"Yes, but Ambassador Choi, the wave of human tide before us is moving at such a pace that failure to respond will escalate the problem. The DMZ has already come down and movement across what little border exist is continuous. This movement can spark a Tuberculosis crisis in Asia," said Ambassador Shackle from the United Kingdom.

The French Ambassador brought his hand up to his forehead. "I propose that we immediately let Japan handle the Tuberculosis issue. They are simply the best with medical humanitarian assistance."

Cherniss saw the nods from all the heads of the member states at the table. "Fine, the Japanese can handle the TB situation."

"It is odd that decisions made in this room affect South Korea and they are not even on the Security Council, as is the absence of Japan," U.S. Ambassador Yeva Schur stated. "Therefore, it is imperative that ROK (Republic of Korea) will maintain the overall leading role in unification."

"Ambassador, why of course ROK will play a prominent role, but let me remind you that reunification does not equate to regime change. This is not only Russia and China's view but is the view of the majority in the General Assembly, which has 193 members."

"The United States views Kim Chul moo as a criminal and thug and will not facilitate putting him in a position to lead the entire peninsula. We will be forced to abstain from voting," Schur said.

On hearing this, Cherniss experienced the thrill of a predator pouncing on prey. His head pounded and throbbed; a large drop of sweat rolled slowly down the center of his back. "Ambassador, do you represent the views of the United States or your personal views? President Obama will address the UN General Assembly tomorrow, prior to the vote to repeal Resolution 82, as if he is the grand architect of reunification of the peninsula. I am beginning to believe there is the Obama way, the highway, or the way of various senators and diplomats; and this is true in-regards to other issues, like Ukraine and Iran."

"Let us not stray from what our purpose is, which to make recommendations to the General Assembly. Only the General Assembly can repeal a resolution and tomorrow's vote will be historic. However, in many ways it demonstrates the meddling in Korea, meddling over decades and decades by major powers. Korea has been one nation for hundreds of years and was divided at the 38th Parallel by this body in 1950. Now the Korean people are saying borders and ideology do not separate them—we are Korean!" Ambassador Shackle continued, "Nuclear weapons? What are our recommendations?"

"Well, we are all in consensus on the mandate for the elimination of WMD (Weapons of Mass Destruction). Is that my understanding?" Cherniss asked.

"Yes, China believes this may be the most beneficial arrangement of a unified Korea. That is, the elimination of WMD from the peninsula will keep Japan and other Asian Countries out of the game. China is insistent that the US military not move forces north on a WMD mission," Ambassador Choi pointed out. His face turned red.

"And vice-versa, Ambassador, China does not move troops south on the pretext of securing WMD," Schur firmly stated back. "The United States refers the SIASJ (Situations in Areas Surrounding Japan under the 1997 Defense Guidelines) Declaration to the General Assembly."

"One crisis that China foresaw with the collapse of North Korea is massive refugee outflows. That does not seem to be occurring and China is grateful for this," Choi said. He now considered it a huge past mistake by his leaders in ignoring the famines over the years in North Korea. China experienced its own huge famine in 1960, and learned from it by launching the Cultural Revolution. *The United States gained an upside on China by airlifting food into Osan, thus gaining political capital from a self-imposed disaster*, Choi thought, *the Americans must have received intel from the South Koreans.*

"Anymore concerns? We have gone over the same issues over and over. A memorandum will be drafted to the General Assembly. In all honesty, I think only time will resolve issues on the peninsula." Cherniss let out a long, tortured sigh, and glared at Yeva Schur.

She knew the question that Cherniss wanted an answer to and it did not involve the Korean peninsula. *Where was her twin sister, Olena Loboda?*

The answer was simple: she didn't know.

Chapter 27

Camp Humphreys

September 28, 2014

The deputy chief of the Russian space agency saw the helicopters from the Russian imaging satellite, *Kosmos-2486*, the latest, most sophisticated Russian spy satellite. He immediately notified Vladimir Putin. At two-thirty in the morning, Korean time, Putin called Chul moo on his direct secure-line.

"The Americans are going to steal my money!" Putin yelled into the phone, as soon as he heard what he thought was Chul moo's voice.

There followed a few seconds of silence. Then: "What? The *Green Dog*?"

"Helicopters from Camp Humphreys are on their way to the *Green Dog* to steal my money. They will be there in minutes. I want you to sink it with a sub!" Sink it!"

"I'm on it," the Russian voice impersonator said and hung up.

Sam Young was awoken by mansion security. While at the Ryongsong Residence, he relinquished his personal security detail and relied on mansion security. The twenty-four year old Russian linguist told him about the call from Putin. "Fine, you did an excellent job! Now go back to bed while I contact the People's navy."

Twenty-five minutes later, Sam woke up the Vice-Marshal of the Navy and issued a direct order to immediately sink the *Green Dog* with submarines in the Yellow Sea.

Accomplishing what was called a sling operation, twenty helicopters, ten CH-47's and ten HH-60's, used a sling with a hook to secure one "black plastic" pallet by sling and fly away. The aircraft were assigned to the 3rd Battalion, 2nd Aviation Regiment, the Army's top-notch aviators from Camp Humphreys.

Watching a live video uplink, Putin watched $16 billion fly east toward Seoul. He even checked his watch, a wasted gesture that Defense Minister Sergei Shoigu saw. "In twenty-two minutes my money is gone. Americans are the biggest crooks in the world!"

"Yes, nothing new." The defense minister's objection was somewhat quieter than Putin's. "Vladimir," began the defense minister cautiously, "there seems to be a problem. It looks like the ship's crew is boarding the last helicopter. Somehow they must know the ship will sink? Perhaps a leak in the message to the sub crews."

Putin stared at the video-link in disbelief. "Let's watch and see what happens."

Shoigu nodded. The two continued watching without comment. Within minutes torpedoes struck the ship. It looked like a series of explosions, each more powerful than the next, sinking the giant ship, bow first in less than four minutes, while Putin and Shoigu watched. All that remained was the smoke from the *Green Dog* billowing in an acrid cloud over the Yellow Sea.

A minute later the *Kosmos* focused its infrared cameras on Yongsan Garrison in the heart of Seoul. These images were immediately cross-loaded to a communications satellite, and from there beamed down to the antenna farm at the 821st Main Space Intelligence Centre, near Moscow. From there they went via fiber-optic line to the Kremlin. *Kosmos* focused its attention on the helicopters as they dropped the pallets onto flatbed trucks assigned to the 25th Transportation Battalion from Camp Humphreys. It happened so fast, the dropping off of pallets and the trucks driving away with armed escort by the Heon-byeong, the ROK Military Police, Putin could only react with a twisting, tightening movement of his body. The trucks entered a tunnel on Myeongdong Street and the satellite visual was lost. The vehicles drove into the entrance of one of the largest underground network of streets. There, they were met by Security Officers from the Bank of Seoul and the transfer was completed. Using a secret underground tunnel, the officers moved the "Black Plastic" to the vault under the Bank of Seoul. The first billions in financial assistance from the United States for the unification of Korea was delivered.

"Where are all the helicopters?" Shoigu asked Putin. "That was only the Chinooks. Where are the Blackhawks?"

"Son of a Bitch," Putin breathed. But the *Kosmos* was answering the questions, and it found the Blackhawks moving east.

"They are going to Japan. We can scramble fighters from Vladivostok and shoot them down over the Sea of Japan."

Putin's head was spinning, the pain in his temples throbbed. "No, the Americans, Japanese, and Koreans are not playing by any rules. Well, from here on we play by new rules."

The sinking of the *Green Dog* set off activity under the sea that Putin and *Kosmos* did not see. The sinking was viewed by Japan as a clear provocation in international waters and the peninsula was surrounded by Japanese Soryu-class attack submarines. Sumiko Albright interpreted the North Korean submarine fleet as an unpredictable wild-card in the entire unification equation. The People's Navy processed ten obsolete Soviet-era Golf-class submarines. Out of the ten, one was seaworthy and undergoing sea trials in the Sea of Japan. In addition, the Peoples' Navy operated Sang-O-Class submarines and small midget submarines around the peninsula. The Command and Control Communication System to the submarine commanders was poor, to say the least, and the commander's had the authority to fire at will if determined Korea was in jeopardy. The North Korean commander of a submarine operates and fights his ship through a surprising lack of chain of command. These submarines were a strategic nightmare for Japan.

The North Korean captain of *Polaris-1*, the Russian Golf-class sub, decided to use the diesel engine rather than the blower to ventilate the ship, which did the job in about half the time. He was at a depth of 200 feet, ten miles off the east coast from its home port of Sinpo South Shipyard. He just completed a test of the seals around the SBLM (submarine ballistic launched missile) tubes when he heard the muffled crump of the impact from the Japanese torpedo. The *Polaris-1*, the pride and joy of the late Kim Jong un, tilted, taking on water fast. Another torpedo hit the *Polaris-1*. In six minutes, the entire crew was dead at the bottom of the Sea of Japan. Within eight minutes of the sinking of the *Polaris-1*, nine other North Korean submarines met a similar fate. It happened that fast. The sky was clear and the sea was calm and no one would have known that a record of ten submarines sunk in eight minutes was just set. The sheer helplessness of the People's Navy against the Soryu-class submarines from Japan.

In his head, Sam Young sang out the Gordon Lightfoot tune, *The Wreck of the Edmond Fitzgerald*, over and over.

Chapter 28

Night Drop

September 29, 2014

It happened with a swiftness that stunned the CMF Watch Commander. The Asbestos Removal Unit completed the work in S-3. After weeks of round-the-clock removal the job was over. Chul moo left CMF the same way he arrived, in a blue, plastic 55 gallon barrel in the middle of the night.

Twenty minutes later, an obedient Chul moo stepped out of the barrel onto the concrete floor of the Cathedral, next to the Flight-line at Travis AFB. He was calm; he'd been given a light sedative, and he was relaxed, his breathing easy.

"Mr. Kim, we are flying you back to Korea. Kim Jong un is dead. There has been a change in Leadership but your country awaits your arrival. Your good friend, Vladimir Putin, secured the release with the UN," Art Morris continued. "We have made all the arrangements. Bubby and Chris will go on the plane with you."

"Okay, Chul moo, we are going to put your jewelry on for the plane ride. We will take the restraints off when we get close to your country," Bubby said.

Standing in one spot, shuffling from side to side and rocking his head, Chul moo moved toward Bubby and turned his back to him. Bubby handed him the waist restraints, and Chul moo wrapped it around his waist and waited for Bubby to adjust the tightness and secure a small padlock to the restraints. Chul moo then placed his own hands in the restraints and tightened them. After Bubby inserted a restraint key into a pin hole to double lock the restraints, preventing them from further tightening, Chul moo spoke. "I like the mango drinks. Can you get some mango drinks for the flight?"

"The 'mighty mango.' I knew that is your favorite and I brought some," Chris Youngblood replied. Chul moo took a few steps forward and kneeled on a small bench while Bubby put Ankle Restraints on him.

"Come on," Chris coaxed. "Let us get on the van so we can drive to the plane."

"Who is in charge? Who is running the country?" Chul moo asked, while stepping into the blue Air Force panel truck. He began to laugh.

Watching him laugh, Art pulled the door closed.

"Dave Chen." Art and Dave shook hands. Art held Chen's hand a little longer than necessary so that he could get a feel for the importance he'd placed on him in the agency. They had spent the last ten or so years working together out of the San Francisco Reserve on Market Street. It had been a fine life, but as the Kim criminal empire grew the trouble at the Fed started; that was when his neat black-and-white life began to fill with various shades of 'supernotes.' "You know I used to get the creeps coming to Travis. It don't bother me anymore."

"Art, you are a part of Air Force history. There should be a statue of you in that Air Museum just up the street from here," Chen said.

He looked at him, speechless. "How's that?"

"For one, the race riots you were involved here at Travis paved the way for a better Air Force. It didn't stop there. As the first black PJ, you cut the path for blacks in Pararescue and Combat Control. I remember hearing the stories about a how they left your ass in the cold water longer than need be, just to fuck with you."

Art smiled. It lit up his whole face. "I did get shit on. But I learned from the past and moved forward. I always tell myself, yesterday is OVER and time to build on a positive future."

"Hey, Chul moo looks like a new man," Chen said vaguely, changing the subject.

"He is not. He is the same evil monster, just heavily medicated. He will stay like that until about six hours or so after he arrives on North Korean soil. I am not aware of your mission specifies. But I will say be careful and get the hell out North Korea ASAP. Your mission will create a positive future for millions. Koreans will have something positive in their future. Your gear is loaded on the jet. Security Police will take you to your bird."

There was a long pause. And although Chen did not know it, Art restrained, with a great—almost heroic—effort, not to embrace Chen. Then Chen stepped into the passenger seat of the Security Police utility vehicle. As the vehicle backed out of the hangar, Chen felt a wave of emotion from the past wash over him. A voice buried somewhere deep in his mind, the voice from his youth, spoke up briefly but clearly to Art: "HOOYAH! PJ ALL THE WAY!"

"HOOYAH!" Art cried, laughing.

It was a beautiful sight to see, even in the dark. The Flight-line at Travis AFB with the rows of KC-10s, C-5s, and C-17s. Clearly, a large portion of the nation's airlift bedded down at Travis. Chen felt his age looking out at the Flight-line. He remembered when there were rows of C-141's on the ramp. Now the only C-141, the Golden Bear, was on display by the red light where he turned right, toward Base Ops and the Flight-line. And up the hill from the Golden Bear was what used to be the Base Hospital, now renovated into offices. As an Airman, Chen worked in the Emergency Room at the Hospital, receiving trauma training. He could still picture the six-foot four master sergeant medic that trained him. It was not the medical training that he still recalled, but the stories of the race riots the sergeant told him about. The sergeant was working in the ER in May of 1971 when the injuries, and one death, poured into the Travis ER from the fighting that broke out in the dormitories. *Time to give this shit up,* Chen thought, *and here I am at age fifty-seven going on an unprecedented jump mission. Not as an Air Force Reservist, but as an employee of the Federal Reserve.* The counterfeit division of the Federal Reserve was a blacker than black ultra-secret organization, it answered to no government agency with no connection whatsoever to the intelligence community. Less than a handful of people knew his role on tonight's mission.

Twelve hours after takeoff, and after two air refueling with a KC-10 Tanker, the C-17 was over North Korean airspace. Sam was allowing aircraft flying China earthquake relief missions to over-fly through North Korean airspace. For the past four days, the Air Defenses were shut down over North Korea. In addition, the entire North Korea military was unraveling with the soon to happen unification. The Air Force took no chances and included an aerial cavalry of ferocious front-line air muscle with the C-17: Two F-22's, an E-3 AWACS, two EA-6B Prowlers, and three KC-135 Tankers.

"He looks like a happy camper now," Bubby said, after Chris fitted a harness over Chul Moo's black Mao style suit.

"Yea, thanks to the injection," Chris replied. "Chul moo, it has been a joy working with you. I never made so much overtime in my life."

Chul moo's eyes locked on the red lights of the C-17 cargo compartment.

At 0255 hours, Sam Young was outside, in the open and all alone on the Ryongsong rooftop helipad landing zone. He placed an IR (infrared) strobe light in the center of the **X** and surrounded it in a sixty foot diameter circle with ten IR Cyalume Chem Light Sticks.

Wearing a MT-1X Parachute over a Ryongsong Mansion Guard uniform, Chen came up behind Chul moo and snapped into his harness. He cinched the four straps as tight as possible to aid in a stable freefall tandem parachute jump. He felt the aircraft entering into a tight spiraling combat descent to 15,000 feet. The loadmaster opened the ramp and Chen held tight as he moved closer to the edge of the ramp. Chul moo was so frightened that his knees buckled and the loadmaster assisted Chen toward the end of the ramp. Chen drew strength and energy from the blackness and altitude, while it was robbing Chul moo of his vitality. With the eagerness of a man being released from a cage, Chen focused on the red jump light, waiting for it to turn green. He could feel the effects of decreased oxygen, but knew he would exit the aircraft momentarily. The light turned green; Chen exited off the ramp into the blackness, arching his back in a hard arch. He immediately assumed a stable position and saw the perimeter lights of Ryongsong Mansion. He was not wearing night-vision googles and could not see the IR strobe and Chem lights. After fifty-five seconds of freefall, Chen pulled his ripcord D-Handle. The opening shock and drastic reduction of airspeed came as a great relief to Chul moo. The two were under canopy, 1800 feet directly above the mansion. Chen pulled his right steering toggle all the way down and entered into a corkscrew descent with very little forward motion. He accomplished a perfect stand-up landing on the helipad **X**.

"You never miss do you?" Sam said as he helped gather the parachute.

"Piece of cake. Just like San Diego," Chen replied. Chen and Sam Young parachuted into Qualcomm Stadium at the 1998 World Series.

"You are my twin brother!" Chul Moo said, his eyes so wide it seemed they must tumble from their sockets. The feverish intensity in his eyes made the expression on his face look like a madman. He suddenly had an all-too-clear picture of what was happening: a Federal Reserve agent posing as his double in North Korea. He attempted to attack Sam but was still restrained with the harness attached to Chen.

Chen tripped Chul moo and hunkered down on top of him. He held Chul moo's arms to prevent his using them. "There is a syringe taped to my right leg. Use it!"

Sam found the syringe. "Sorry, brother, I would have liked to talk, but it does not look like that is going to happen." Sam lifted Chul moo's shirt and injected the needle into the flesh on his right side. Chul moo bared his teeth as he bucked and twisted while he faded into unconsciousness.

They made their way through secret passageways, Sam in the lead with Chul moo over his shoulders and Chen trailing behind. Sam laid Chul moo down in the bed. He checked his watch, 0320 hours.

"How the hell do we get out of here?" Chen asked.

"The escape tunnels are based on a simple number system, that is, knowing the right turns to take. It is like a maze and one could get lost for days. The tunnels will get us to the river."

By 0430 hours, after moving through a series of escape tunnels, Sam and Chen emerged by the Kim Il sung Square, next to the banks of the Taedong River, in the rain. Fifteen hundred years ago the Koguryo Kingdom was founded on the shores of the Taedong and an ever-patient Korean people extended their aristocratic state north and south. They felt the heavy drops on their cheeks and entered the river as the downpour started. Both wore 1/8" chicken vest wet suits under their clothes that helped with buoyancy and the cold water. The swim was a slow breast stroke west toward the Yellow Sea.

There was pandemonium at Ryongsong Mansion. Chul moo burst breathlessly out of his room, down the stairs, and through a side door that opened directly to the courtyard.

"Escape! There has been an escape!" Chul moo shouted. He had expected to find a colonel or general or two from the People's Army after he shouted, but there was no one.

Lee and the Head of Mansion Security arrived at the same time. "Lee, I am glad to see you! I was kidnapped and just returned to North Korea by parachute. The saboteurs are in the mansion or within Pyongyang. They must be found! Where are my weapons?"

Lee, like the security chief, had that one moment, as he listened to Chul moo rant and rave, when he was wandering if Chul moo had lost his mind.

Sirens blared, guards rushed throughout the compound, dogs barked, and the Pyongyang Police were alerted. The city was full of military due to the official unification announcement by Kim Chul moo scheduled for the afternoon.

After swimming past two bridges, they saw lights start popping on in the darkened city. A siren echoed over Pyongyang. Something nudged both swimmers softly, and seconds later two bottlenose dolphins, *Jake* and *Jerry* appeared. *Jake* was a twenty-eight year old dolphin assigned with the U.S. Navy MK-8 unit, the most classified unit in the military. *Jerry* was a ten-year old dolphin trained by *Jake*. *Jake*, a Persian Gulf veteran, in the past performed missions solo. The trainers at MK-8 discovered that a dolphin alone is not really a dolphin. The dolphin's social network system is so complex that *Jake* performed better with other male dolphins, and he essentially trained the younger dolphins. Taking in a lungful of air, Sam grabbed *Jake's* Dorsal fin, and *Jake* dove with Sam to a "parked" AURV (Advanced Underwater Remotely Piloted Vehicle) on the river bottom. Unable to see, Sam felt around and found the full-face mask and secured it around his face. He followed the oxygen line to its attachment point on the AURV and pressed a button. He raised his head and tilted the bottom of the mask as the initial surge of air purged the water from the mask. Positioning himself in the left seat, Sam glanced to his right and barely could barely distinguish Chen situating himself in the right seat. Sam pushed a rubber button, activating the AURV, and five seconds later the vehicle glided through the water back toward what the Japanese called "Home Plate," the Soryu-class submarine, the *Jinryu*. On board the two men rode exposed to the water, breathing from the AURV's rebreather unit that left no telltale trail of bubbles like regular scuba equipment. Seventy minutes later, in the first available deep water, the AURV operator in the *Jinryu* eased the vehicle into a gentle docking on the back of the *Jinryu*. Three divers exited the *Jinryu* and assisted Sam and Chen to the lock-in/lock-out chamber.

Chapter 29

Unification

October 1, 2014

Luke Young was smiling. And when he smiled, he resembled Paul Newman. If this would have been a few months earlier, Kim's cronies that made their living from what few tourist that visited would have kept an eye on him day and night. He was surprised that no one took interest in an old Caucasian man, but then again this was the biggest day ever for Koreans and the entire city mobilized on Juche Square. What was the most restricted city in the world now appeared to have no restrictions. Wearing jogging shoes, sweat pants, a Yankees Baseball cap, and a Nike sweat shirt that read, *Just Do it*, he entered the sixth floor of the hotel from the stairwell. The entire sixth floor was under renovation and had been for the past four years. As expected, room 669 was unlocked. He entered the room, locked the door, and spend several minutes just standing, listening, and studying the room. When no sounds came he moved to a vent located on the wall next to the floor. He twisted a small notch securing the vent; the vent failed to open, and he removed his glove and used it like a cloth wrench to turn the notch--The vent opened. Luke withdrew a 91/30 Mosin-Nagant rifle with a PU Sniper Scope wrapped in a sheet. Unwrapping the rifle from the sheet he discovered one five-round stripper clip loaded with what he knew contained the most advanced *boat-tail* high-velocity bullet ever developed. Lovingly and meticulously he inspected the rifle--testing the bolt action, trigger squeeze, breech and barrel, and lower portion of the stock. Finally, he loaded the rifle using the stripper clip. Using the bolt action, he inserted a bullet into the chamber. He looked out the window from the room and barely saw a small portion of Juche Square, approximately 1000 yards or a little over half a mile to the elevated podium, because of obstructions from other buildings. He unclipped the window lock and slid the window open. Four feet back from the window, he raised the rifle to his shoulder and squinted through the telescope. The podium in the square beyond the window a half-mile away came into focus. Due to many obstructions and buildings, all he could see in the line of fire was the podium and a few feet around it. The head of a man preparing for the forthcoming ceremony passed across the scope's reticle. He sighted on the head with the scope. The head appeared large and clear, as large as a balloon at his granddaughter's birthday.

Satisfied at last, he checked his Breitling *Superocean* watch. He had ten minutes until Chul moo was scheduled to speak. Eight minutes later, Luke Young, from a standing position, raised the rifle to the firing position. He held the rifle very steady and squinted down the telescopic sight. He could see Billy Becker quite clearly, the red hair, freckles, and nose-ring, preparing to introduce Chul moo. He saw Chul moo come up to the podium, the crossed reticles of the sight were centered on the bridge of the nose, between the eyes. *I'll give him a minute to get his message out.* Keeping the rifle on target, Luke waited—then, softly, gently, he squeezed the trigger. . . .

A split second later he saw Chul moo's head explode as he rocked back from the podium. Luke saw enough. He wrapped the sheet around the rifle and placed it back into the vent. He was excited but calmed down while walking down the stairwell. The walk toward the hotel helped relax him even more, despite the wail of the sirens, growing louder, all around him. He expected the Police to converge on him, arrest him, and execute him within days. In fifteen minutes he joined his tour group at the hotel and listened to their version of the assassination.

"Holy Mary Mother of God," the seventy-year old woman from Minnesota said softly. "It was a slaughterhouse in the Square. The President was shot in the head and when he fell backwards the assassin rushed the stage and put more bullets into him, then the bodyguards gunned down the assassin."

"That's when we decided to get the hell out of there and return to the hotel," the old woman's husband said.

"I was standing not too far from you two and saw the same thing," Luke said with conviction. "I just hope the game tonight is not cancelled. That is the only reason I booked this trip."

"I told you we should stay away from these third world countries. Too dangerous!"

"Excuse me. I am going to shower and change. I'm kinda sweaty from the jog/walk I did around the city." With a smart nod, Luke turned away.

Chapter 30

A Talk in the Office

October 15, 2015

Mike Perry and TJ Hill had watched the assassination on CNN from Mike's Office. The Director understood. When the last Kim fell, the entire Kim regime and criminal empire fell with him. According to the UN reunification plan, the successor of the newly united Korea became Park Geun-hye. The second gunman was a surprise to Director Perry. It was a stroke of good luck.

TJ stared at Mike for a long time, as if reflecting on many things, wandering the unknown.

"What happened to the printing press that produced all the PBFs in country?" TJ asked.

"The Federal Reserve acquired it. Something about asset protection."

"Asset Protection?"

Mike listened to him without answering the question, realizing TJ earned a response. "I guess so. I don't know. It is all out of my pay grade. The dollar is now backed by gold."

"Good. Then something decent, something benefiting the United States, came out of this whole Office 39 madness."

"Maybe, but don't count on it. Putin is pissed. He had intentions of ending the ruble crisis by taking Russia onto the gold standard—North Korean gold. So he goes 'balls to the wall' into Ukraine."

"I think Russia would have gone into Ukraine anyway, full-scale no matter what."

"One bad guy down and another one steps up his own evil. Our focus is now Ukraine and Eastern Europe. I think we are going to have our hands full."

"Yea, well, the days of the Kim regime are over."

Epilogue

The Chess Player

March 9, 2015

Out of the two Malaysian airliner incidents; out of a dead dictator and intelligence operatives; out of the unification of the Korean peninsula, a chapter of events was added to the sum of minor human history.

The sky was grey and the sun barely shined on the grave of Chess Champion Bobby Fisher. For the two men standing over the grave, in the small churchyard of Laugardaelir, the secret meeting place, the situation seemed better now, the cold rain had stopped. A ceiling of grey clouds one thousand feet over their heads, blown along by twenty-knot winds toward Iceland's city of Selfoss, the only major city not located on the Icelandic coastline. In the churchyard the snow was sparse, dirty white, only lately melted, littered with the small volcanic rocks, in the distance some as much as three feet high, a landscape that broke up shapes. Proof of the earth's dynamics. The two men meeting was proof of the dynamics of the human-the dynamics of conflict.

TJ knew the man he was about to talk with only by his code-name, the chess player; a man that secretly sought out this meeting with the CIA. But in seeing him, TJ realized his identity, a chess champion himself. His name was on the tip of his tongue but he could not remember it.

"About as light as it is going to get," TJ said. The light level was what meteorologists called nautical twilight and it was two in the afternoon.

Bundled in a coat, the chess player walked to the tombstone and knelt down. Unfolding his arms, opening his coat, exposing himself to the chill, he removed a small bundle of white and black roses, the color of chess pieces. "He would be seventy-two today had he lived," he said, "he died at age sixty-four, one year on earth for each square on a chess board."

"He was a great chess player, Perhaps the greatest that ever lived. There may be a greater player still alive," TJ said, revealing his astonishment of the man before him.

The chess player stood and faced TJ. "So you know who I am?"

"Yes."

"I ask that you not reveal my identity," the chess player said, realizing the man still had not used the "password story," the story that would authenticate who he was. *I am such an amateur*, he thought.

There was a flash of something—TJ did not know what; fear, perhaps—in the chess player's eyes. "I met a man. I don't know who he was and we talked. You have my word." TJ extended his hand and the two shook hands.

They looked at each other and the chess player's doubts vanished. "Fisher stopped playing when he was twenty-nine. He reached his peak in Iceland, 1972, Fisher vs. Spassky and that year was the pinnacle of popularity for chess."

"It is funny. You can call it what you may, fate, luck, or destiny, but as a young man I camped just a hundred yards from here in a one-man tent. I was stationed at the NATO base in Keflavik. On a four-day weekend, I hitchhiked to Selfoss. It was summertime, and I was dropped off at this spot. I thought it was the most peaceful, beautiful place I had ever seen. The church surrounded by the green meadows, the volcanic rocks, and the mountain in the background. In the morning, I sat on an insulite pad by my tent, drinking coffee, and said, "God grant every man such a view."

This was the "password story" and the chess player conveyed a great deal more about the old man. He believed the story was true. "Yes, and I believe the same peace you felt when you were here was felt by Bobby Fisher. That is why he wanted to rest here. He saw the same thing you did."

TJ reminisced as he looked out toward where he camped some forty years ago. "Are you satisfied?"

His voice was tiny, almost delicate, but nevertheless—

In front of TJ, the chess player said, "This is Boris Nemtsov's Pamphlet. He was killed for the information in it . . . information that goes to the heart of the Putin Pillar of Power—the lie. Putin is infuriated over the unification of Korea. He feels he was snookered on Korea." He thrust a wrapped box into TJ's chest. It looked like a gift, a box of chocolate or something.

Afterwards, the chess player froze, as if aware of the implications of his action. He couldn't have stood frozen for long—when he regained control of his thoughts. What brought him out of it was the cold rain and wind hitting his face. "There is a digital recording on a flash drive of a meeting. It details Putin's knowledge/involvement concerning the two Malaysian airliners, his ties to the previous Kim criminal empire, along with a possible future plot with an airliner in Europe," he said in a trembling, low voice. "There is a contact, a woman that must be found. She has a plan to take out the Black Sea Fleet in Crimea."

TJ was interested. "A woman?"

And, after five or ten endless seconds he spoke. "Yes, a Ukrainian woman. She must be found before the Russians find her. . . Bobby Fisher annihilated his opponents with outlandish, bold moves. This woman can annihilate Putin's navy with her bold, daring move." The chess player hugged his coat more tightly to his chest. His heart, which had begun to slow down, like after making a winning chess move that would force his opponent to resign. The heart thumping harder than ever prior to the move. "Your move."

He began to smile. He was still smiling two minutes later, as he shrugged into his coat and stepped into a white Toyota sedan and drove away.

About the Author

David Joseph is a veteran Air Force Flyer. While in the Air Force, he flew on the HH-53, HH-3, HC-130, C-141, and KC-10 aircraft, and traveled to every continent in the world. His travels and experiences provide unlimited material for writing.

He is the author of *Korea x 2*, *Silent Six*, and *Putin's Gold*, a military thriller Trilogy, set on the Korean peninsula, *The Bully & Other Stories*, and the two best-selling novelettes, *The Great Hijacking* and *Putin's Shoot-down!* He is currently writing a short story collection called *Stories From The Abyss* and a novel about expelling the Russians from Crimea. He holds a Master of Arts in Military Studies from American Military University.

"I have twenty short stories and three novels in my head!"